Latino Immigrants in the United States

Immigration and Society series

Christian Joppke, *Citizenship and Immigration*

Ronald L. Mize and Grace Peña Delgado, *Latino Immigrants in the United States*

Philip Q. Yang, *Asian Immigration to the United States*

Latino Immigrants in the United States

Ronald L. Mize and Grace Peña Delgado

polity

First published in 2012 by Polity Press

Polity Press
65 Bridge Street
Cambridge CB2 1UR, UK

Polity Press
350 Main Street
Malden, MA 02148, USA

ISBN-13: 978-0-7456-4742-5
ISBN-13: 978-0-7456-4743-2(pb)

A catalogue record for this book is available from the British Library.

Typeset in 11 on 13 pt Sabon
by Servis Filmsetting Ltd, Stockport, Cheshire
Printed and bound in Great Britain by the MPG Books Group

The publisher has used its best endeavors to ensure that the URLs for external websites referred to in this book are correct and active at the time of going to press. However, the publisher has no responsibility for the websites and can make no guarantee that a site will remain live or that the content is or will remain appropriate.

Every effort has been made to trace all copyright holders, but if any have been inadvertently overlooked the publisher will be pleased to include any necessary credits in any subsequent reprint or edition.

For further information on Polity, visit our website: www.politybooks.com

Contents

List of Tables and Figures

Preface: In the Shadows of América Tropical

The images on the cover of this book represent two opposing views of Mexicans in Los Angeles. Olvera Street, a marketplace replete with restaurants and curio shops, was originally founded in 1926 by Christine Sterling, an English-born, Progressive Era reformer and philanthropist. Mexican culture, Sterling contended, could be made both modern and profitable if sufficiently sanitized. Olvera Street represents Sterling's vision of the role that Mexicans would play in both the history and the future of Los Angeles: one of consumption and invisibility. An indirect yet poignant critique of Sterling's vision of Olvera Street and the treatment of Mexicans in the United States came from exiled Mexican muralist David Alfaro Siqueiros in *América Tropical*. The work, which was painted at the Olvera Street Plaza Art Center in 1932, prominently featured an indigenous *campesino* (farmer) crucified under the gaze of an American bald eagle. Taking aim at the eagle were two armed revolutionaries. The contrasting perspectives of Sterling and Siqueiros inform the analytical framework of *Latino Immigrants in the United States*. While early twentieth-century apprehensions at Olvera Street consisted primarily of Mexican–Anglo tensions, a similar mistrust came to define relationships between other Latino immigrants and white Americans well into the twenty-first century. The causes and consequences of these centuries-long apprehensions – nativism, US foreign policy in Latin America, worker exploitation, urbanization, and political resistance – are among the themes explored in this book.

* * *

Los Angeles is home to the largest Mexican-origin population outside of Mexico City, while simultaneously hosting more than 1 million Latino immigrants from Central and South America. Los Angeles also is home to the second largest concentration of Salvadorans behind the capital of San Salvador and has more Central Americans residing there than any other US city (Hamilton and Chinchilla 2001: 41). Los Angeles is the quintessential global city where key transnational corporations and the global entertainment industry are headquartered. On full display throughout affluent Los Angeles is a consumer society that drives globalization by fetishizing conspicuous consumerism as a way of life. Rarely acknowledged are the immigrants who toil in the shadows to serve those who benefit from the spoils of the global economy. The increasingly informal economy that employs the new serving classes of undocumented workers (Sassen 2005) is marked by under-the-radar jobs, wages paid in cash or bartering, and a lack of safeguards and protections against unscrupulous employment practices.

The idealized image of a Mexican marketplace in the foreground on the cover represents one imposed on Latinos in the popular imagination that is often related to tourist consumption (Mize and Swords 2010; Swords and Mize 2008). The origins of Olvera Street began in 1926, when Sterling, an affluent English immigrant who had recently relocated to Los Angeles from San Francisco, focused her philanthropy on modernizing the original Mexican settlements near downtown Los Angeles. The oldest structure in Los Angeles, the Francisco Avila Adobe house, was like most of Olvera Street, in disrepair and dilapidated. The area of town was called Sonoratown because of the large population of Mexicans originating from the state of Sonora, although Italians, Greeks, Germans, Irish, and Chinese, among others, also resided in the *barrio* or neighborhood (Lewthwaite 2009: 37). In many ways, what became Olvera Street represented what Anglos like Sterling preferred to see as a Mexican culture fixed in the past in a pristine state, a Mexico of yesterday designed for Anglo tourist consumption but in no way connected to modern Los Angeles. Postcards from the 1930s to 1970s variously referred to Olvera Street as "Little Mexico," "Old Mexico," and "A Mexican Street of Yesterday, in a City of Today."[1]

Today, the area is known as El Pueblo de Los Angeles (City of Los Angeles) Historic Monument and encompasses the city's first church (*Iglesia de la Placita*), restored residences of Californian elite such as Pio Pico and Eloisa Martinez de Sepulveda, the larger Plaza that was actually used by Mexicans in the area as a gathering and shopping place, and Italian Hall. Yet, it is Olvera Street and its "authentic Mexican market" that strikes a chord in the American popular imagination, most often because it reproduces many stereotypes of Mexicans that have persisted since Sterling's initial efforts to sequester the influence of Mexican culture on Angelenos to one city block stuck in a mythic past. Just two blocks away, in the adjacent Plaza, a wholesale removal of a Mexican presence is reproduced by a historical amnesia concerning the forgotten events known as the Great Repatriation. The Depression-era repatriation program impacted Mexican communities throughout the United States but many of the most egregious mass round up and deportation methods were applied in Los Angeles.

> Perhaps the most celebrated razzia [raid] was the infamous La Placita raid, which occurred on February 26, 1931.... The police immediately posted two officers at each entrance to La Placita to prevent anyone from escaping. The suddenness of the action caught people completely by surprise. A sense of panic swept through the crowd. This type of raid was different from those conducted in business places, where suspected illegals were apprehended individually. A wholesale raid in a public park was something new. (Balderrama and Rodríguez 2006: 73)

Sanchez (1993: 210) estimates that Los Angeles lost one-third of its Mexican population as a result of the repatriation program. The repatriation campaigns eventually led nationwide to the forced and voluntary removal of 1 to 2 million Mexicans, regardless of citizenship status.

Today, the original Spanish outpost of *El Pueblo de Nuestra Señora Reina de los Ángeles sobre El Rio Porciuncula*, founded by 44 Spanish colonists in 1781, is now encompassed by the Historic Monument locked in space and time by a memorialization imposed, however inaccurately, on Olvera Street. It is actually the third location of the original *pueblo* after floods washed away the first two Spanish colonial settlements. Trapped in that time-space is a neglected story of interactions between California's indigenous inhabitants and Spanish conquistadores, the recognition of Alta California post-Mexico independence from Spain, the ranching past of the area associated with Avila, Sepulveda, and other inhabitants, and how the area's role as the center of Mexican Los Angeles was displaced due to neglect. As the *pueblo* became home to the most destitute and recent of immigrants from Mexico and Southern and Eastern Europe, the deterioration of the original Mexican Los Angeles continued unabated until two events during the Great Depression era disrupted the downward slide: the immigration raids and deportations from La Plaza during the Great Repatriation and the white appropriation of Olvera Street for tourist consumption of a thoroughly racialized Mexican culture of old – the former relegated to history and the latter still present in contemporary representations of Olvera Street.

Enter into this time of turmoil the prominent Mexican muralist David Alfaro Siqueiros. When Siqueiros was rousted out of his home country in the aftermath of the Mexican Revolution, his brief exile in Los Angeles coincided with the commissioning of a mural to be painted on the second-floor, exterior wall behind Italian Hall on Olvera Street. The title of the mural was the only parameter he was given but the assumption was he would portray a bright, vibrant, colorful "Tropical America" to match the touristy feel of Olvera Street. What Siqueiros unveiled on the evening of October 9, 1932 was an *América Tropical* that prominently featured an indigenous *campesino*, or poor Latin American subsistence farmer, crucified under the watchful eye of a bald eagle. The bald eagle is targeted by two revolutionary peasants, their rifles cocked (this was the most prominent, visible part of the mural from Olvera Street and the first section to be whitewashed by Los

Angeles City reformers). In the background, a pre-Columbian Mexico leitmotif of a Mayan pyramid, Chac-Mool, and other statues are featured with a gnarled, knotted, almost painful rendering of jungle vines framing the mural. Siqueiros was both a product of and actor in the Mexican Revolution. Along with José Clemente Orozco and Diego Rivera, Siqueiros is one of the "Big Three" Mexican artists of the revolution and their images (from public murals to portraits) captured the spirit and politics of the times. After being forced to leave Mexico for his radical politics, his arrival in Los Angeles in 1932 was at a time of his heightened political awareness and thus Siqueiros worked in secrecy to unveil his public criticism of US imperialism in Latin America. He was subsequently deported after his mural was received with shock, disdain, and censure.

The erasure of Latin American and Latino history and Siqueiros' political indictment of US imperialism was accomplished with the whitewashing of the mural. Interestingly, when the Mexican American civil rights movement arose in 1960s Los Angeles, the whitewash started to crack and a resurrection of restoring and conserving *América Tropical* arose during the Chicano Movement. Slated to open in 2012 replete with a cultural interpretive center, the efforts over the past 40 years to return the mural to its former stature and in this regard, those funding the restoration, such as the Getty Conservation Institute and the El Pueblo Historic Monument, have come full circle in supporting the mural they once deplored.

The final image on the cover towers over the serene image of Olvera Street in the form of the alabaster Los Angeles City Hall. It has a long popular recognition due to its display in 1960s television shows such as *Dragnet* and *Perry Mason*. Yet, it is not until 2006 that City Hall takes on its current relevance. The building became inextricably linked to the immigrant rights movement in the newspaper images of millions of protestors surrounding it during what became known as *La Gran Marcha*. On Saturday, March 25, the immigrant rights movement garnered national headlines when immigrants and their supporters took to the streets in cities across the nation. Approximately 1 million people marched in

Los Angeles to denounce the Sensenbrenner Bill, HR 4437, which among several elements would have made it a felony to reside in the United States without legal documentation. This event culminated in a less spontaneous, more organized demonstration, "A Day Without an Immigrant" rallies on May 1, 2006. The title is important as the first iteration was based on the mock documentary and motion picture *A Day Without a Mexican* and progressed to the more inclusive "Day Without a Latino" rally. The final version, "A Day Without an Immigrant," took immigrant rights to its most inclusive form and facilitated coalitions between labor unions and immigrant service providers. The May Day rallies were also coined "The Great American Boycott" as organizers urged immigrants and their supporters not to attend work or to purchase any goods. Many immigrant-serving companies closed in solidarity. Chicano students walked out to join immigrant supporters in a daytime rally in Los Angeles and, combined with an evening rally, together drew approximately 2 million people.

If Sterling thought she could render invisible a contemporary Mexican Los Angeles by presenting an "old Mexico" with a "quaint, primitive culture," Siqueiros' *América Tropical* sought to connect the images and experiences of Mexicans to how Latin America was subsumed by and reacted to US imperialism. Nowhere were these competing definitions of what it means to be Mexican or Latino fought out more clearly than in the United States by those immigrants who left Latin America for a myriad of reasons. In the following chapters, we discuss the rising political power and citizenship claims by Latino immigrants, the continuing role of US foreign policy and its relationship to Latino immigration, and the lingering stereotypes and negative characterizations of Latino immigrants as they seek to find a place in the United States while retaining their transnational ties.

1

Introduction: Latino Immigrants Claiming Rights

When Marcelo Lucero set out for a walk on November 8, 2008 with friend Angel Loja in Patchogue, New York, the 37-year-old immigrant had no idea that his life would be in peril. In 1993, at the age of 21, Lucero, along with his brother Joselo, arrived in the United States from their native Gualaceo, Ecuador, and eventually settled in Riverhead, New York, a Long Island suburb. There, Lucero was employed as a dry-cleaning attendant and earned a reputation as someone who did not complain about his 60-hour work-week schedule. Like many immigrants, Lucero's work ethic was driven by improving the lives of family members abroad by sending remittances, or *migradólares*, to them. Lucero's dedication, however, ended when he became the latest victim in a series of hate crimes targeting Latino immigrants. As Lucero and his friend neared the Patchogue Railroad Station parking lot, they were approached by seven teenage boys and three teenage girls shouting racial slurs at the two "Spanish guys" (Police Department, County of Suffolk, New York 2008a: 2; see also *The New York Times* 2008). The group's deliberate intentions – to go "beat up some beaners" – escalated into a frenzy of gang-style violence that ended in Lucero's death. Lucero was attacked by four teenagers, but the fatal wound was wielded by Jeffrey Conroy, a 19-year-old Patchogue native and a stand-out high-school athlete, who was later convicted of manslaughter for Lucero's fatal stabbing.

The murder of Marcelo Lucero is emblematic of anti-immigrant or nativist violence against Latino immigrants that fueled, for

1

example, the slayings of Chilean students Nicolas Pablo Corp-Torres and Racine Balbontin-Aragondona in Miramar, Florida; Pedro Corzo, a Cuban-born immigrant gunned down in Dateland, Arizona; and Luis Ramírez, a Mexican immigrant, who was beaten to death in Shenandoah, Pennsylvania. The pattern of Latino immigrant murders, according to a study by the Federal Bureau of Investigation (FBI) in 2009, is part of a larger trend in the rise of hate crimes against Latinos which increased 40 percent between 2003 and 2007 (FBI 2009: 3; Semple 2008).[2] Latino immigrants, the study contends, received the brunt of attacks, although their assailants have rarely paused to consider the national origins of their would-be victims. While racially motivated attacks against Latinos are on the rise, civil rights and immigrant rights groups such as the Mexican American Legal and Education Defense Fund (MALDEF), the National Council of La Raza (NCLR), LatinoJustice/Puerto Rican Legal Defense and Education Fund (PRLDEF), the Central American Resource Center (CARECEN), and the Southern Poverty Law Center (SPLC) have mounted considerable legal defense to counter the tide of nativism, including the Lucero case.

When Marcelo Lucero was beaten and then stabbed to death, local officials failed initially to bring charges against the assailants and denied that race played a role in the attack. MALDEF, along with Lucero's family and friends, pressured Suffolk County Executive Attorney Steve Levy not only to prosecute the case, but to charge all of Lucero's seven teenage attackers with a hate crime under New York State's ethnic intimidation law. Soon thereafter, the Suffolk County District Attorney's Office filed murder and ethnic intimidation charges against Conroy, the main perpetrator in Lucero's fatal stabbing. Assistant District Attorney Megan O'Donnell prosecuted the case on behalf of Suffolk County and sketched the manner in which Lucero and Loja were targeted and attacked. In her opening statement, O'Donnell described how the teenagers, including Conroy, roamed Patchogue that fateful Saturday evening "looking for blood – specifically, Mexican blood" (Fernandez 2010a; Police Department, County of Suffolk, New York 2008b). O'Donnell detailed a popular weekend sport called "Mexican-hopping" or "beaner-hopping" that the teenagers were practicing. Their feelings of white supremacy, O'Donnell argued, made Suffolk County Latinos – especially immigrants – "easy targets" because of their ethnicity and isolation.

The Lucero case took nearly two years to prosecute. Conroy, who at time of the trial was 19 years old, and six other teenagers – Christopher Overton, 18, and Jose Pacheco, 19, both from East Patchogue, Jordan Dasch, 19, Anthony Hartford, 19, Nicholas Hausch, 19, and Kevin Shea, 19, all from Medford – were eventually convicted for their role in the fatal stabbing of Marcelo Lucero and the attack on Angel Loja. Conroy was found guilty of manslaughter as a hate crime and was sentenced to 25 years in prison, but not murder in the second degree as a hate crime, a charge that carries a life sentence (Fernandez 2010d, 2010e). Shea, described as the "second-most culpable" of the group, was sentenced to seven years in prison for first-degree gang assault, second-degree attempted assault as a hate crime, and fourth-degree conspiracy (CBS New York 2010; Sorrentino 2010). Pacheco, Dasch, Hartford, and Overton were convicted of first-degree gang assault and attempted assault as a hate crime against Angel Loja. With the exception of Overton, their seven-year prison sentence also included a conviction for attempted assault in the second degree as a hate crime of Hector Sierra and Petronila Fuentes Díaz, a separate attack that took place on the same day as the Lucero and Loja assault (Hesson 2010a; Fernandez 2010c; Buckley 2008; Jabali-Nash 2010). Overton and Hausch received lighter sentences of five years that included punishment for gang assault and conspiracy. These two assailants were not punished for the direct beating and stabbing of Lucero (Hesson 2010b; Fernandez 2010b). The ensuing media coverage highlighted the climate of nativism in Suffolk County, where the so-called Patchogue-7 spread race hatred, intimidation, and violence on a regular basis. In a news conference, District Attorney Thomas Spota detailed for the public several incidents in which Latino immigrants were knocked off their bicycles, cornered and punched in laundromats, or attacked while walking down the street. Some of these individuals were attacked multiple times and on different dates. To underscore the frequency of "beaner-hopping" in Suffolk County, Spota shared a statement made by one of the defendants, presumably in self-defense: "I don't go out doing this very often, maybe once a week" (Brown 2008; Police Department, County of Suffolk, New York 2008c: 3).

The murder of Marcelo Lucero underscores the reality that places like Patchogue can be perilous, if not deadly, for Latino immigrants. Although welcome for their labor and their strong work ethic, Latino immigrants often find themselves the targets of hate crimes in areas of the United States that are otherwise considered bastions of white, middle-class values. But in Patchogue this placid image has been superseded by the town's reputation as a hotbed of nativism where rapid growth in the Latino population has been met by local residents with violence, intimidation, and murder. Between 1980 and 2010, the Latino population on Long Island tripled to nearly 370,000, representing approximately 12 percent of that area's overall population. This rate of growth in the Latino population was far greater than that for the Long Island population as a whole and significantly more rapid than the Latino population growth rate nationwide. In Suffolk and Nassau counties, the Latino population increased from 282,693 in 2000 to 368,430 in 2008. Since 1990, the Latino rate of increase on Long Island has more than doubled at a rate of 123 percent.[3] While the rate of increase nationwide in the Latino population has been substantial over the last ten years, Patchogue and Medford have experienced the most dramatic growth in Latino residents over the last 20 years: in 1990 they comprised 3 percent of the towns' residents while in 2008 Latinos made up approximately 11 percent of the Medford and 24 percent of Patchogue total population (Torras and Skinner 2010). This dramatic growth in the Latino population, especially in Suffolk County (where ironically most Latinos are legal residents or of Puerto Rican descent and therefore citizens of the United States), has been greeted not only with virulent nativism but also a general disregard for the national origins or citizenship status of Latinos. Long Island residents often assume Latinos are foreigners, interlopers born outside the United States. Furthermore, the label of "Mexican" is often attached to someone who merely appears to be of Hispanic descent; the stigma of being "Mexican," in turn, carries with it the assumption of being "illegal" or "alien," a person who is unlawfully in the United States.

The tide of nativism in Patchogue and Medford, and in Suffolk County in general, has taken its heaviest toll on Latinos. They live in fear and, unfortunately, had been so years before the murder of Marcelo Lucero in 2008. In 1998, a militant nativist group called Sachem Quality of Life formed in Farmingville, a small hamlet village of 15,000 residents in Suffolk County, was successful in creating a climate of fear for Long Island Latinos. Over its six-year existence, the nativist group began crafting the image that Latino immigrants were antithetical to local values and posed a considerable threat to the quality of life in Farmingville. Sachem Quality of Life cast Latino immigrants as rapists, thieves, and murderers. The organization also mounted a considerable campaign to prevent day laborers, the most visible and vulnerable segment of the Farmingville Latino population at that time, from finding work and from creating a safe day-labor work site. Political leaders in Suffolk were quick to capitalize on the anti-immigrant sentiments by calling for laws aimed at restricting day laborers who sought work from street corners or in front of home improvement centers. Officials also aimed to restrict immigrants from residing in particular neighborhoods in Farmingville while making no secret of their own nativist sentiment and tacit encouragement of violent acts toward Latino immigrants. Two examples are particularly poignant. In public hearings, first in August 2001 County Legislator Michael D'Andre of Smithtown stated that if day laborers ever entered his town, "We'll be up in arms; we'll be out with baseball bats." County Legislator Elie Mystal of Amityville stated on March 2007: "If I'm living in a neighborhood and people are gathering like that, I would load my gun and start shooting, period. Nobody will say it, but I'm going to say it" (Southern Poverty Law Center 2009: 8). Although Sachem Quality of Life is now defunct, the group, together with the Federation for American Immigration Reform and a smaller nativist group called American Patrol, have influenced the manner in which Latino immigrants were and continue to be received and treated in Suffolk County.

In 2009, the Southern Poverty Law Center (SPLC) documented just how much fear Suffolk County Latino immigrants faced over the last ten years. "They are regularly taunted, spit upon and pelted with apples, full soda cans, beer bottles and other projectiles. Their houses and apartments are egged, spray-painted with racial epithets and riddled with bullets in drive-by shootings." This low-level harassment, according to the SPLC report, often escalated into violence. Immigrants reported that they were shot with BB or pellet guns, or showered in the eyes with pepper spray. Others testified that they were run off the road by cars while riding bicycles and were chased into the woods by drivers while traveling on foot. The SPLC also recorded abundant first-hand accounts of immigrants being punched and kicked by random attackers, beaten with baseball bats, or robbed at knifepoint. From 1998 to 2008, the SPLC documented more than 50 accounts of violence against Latino immigrants on Long Island, activity that local police seemed to ignore. One resident captured the impact of racialized violence on Latino immigrants living in Suffolk County: "We live with the fear that if we leave our houses, something will happen. It's like we're psychologically traumatized from what happens here" (SPLC 2009: 5, 11, 21–8).

However pervasive the climate of fear may be for those living and working in Long Island, the experiences of Latino immigrants is not a story of victimization. Rather, Latino immigrants themselves, with the assistance of immigrant-rights advocates, mounted considerable challenges to discrimination and wanton racism by asserting claims on their civil and human rights. To counter the incidence of hate crimes and rampant nativism in Suffolk County, for example, MALDEF, PRLDEF, the SPLC, the American Civil Liberties Union (ACLU), and numerous immigrant-rights activists assisted in the case against the Patchogue-7 and advocated for the rights of local immigrants. Often the assertion of civil and human rights of immigrants rests on the invocation of the Fourteenth Amendment of the United States Constitution. The Amendment, which was ratified in 1868 during the era of American Reconstruction (1865–77) and prevented the denial of citizenship to freed slaves, asserts the rights of persons living within the United States. Anti-immigrant legislation and discrimination have been successfully countered by reminding lawmakers of the Fourteenth Amendment's legal safeguards for all people in the United States, regardless of citizenship status: "Nor shall any state, deny to any persons within its jurisdiction the equal protection of the laws." In Suffolk County, this advocacy has translated into several developments. At the urging of LatinoJustice/PRLDEF, the Department of Justice, in 2009, launched a criminal investigation into hate crimes in Suffolk County and the manner in which the Suffolk County Police Department has handled the reporting, documentation, and prosecution of hate crimes.

At the grassroots level, Long Island residents formed Neighbors in Support of Immigrants, in part to challenge the tide of anti-immigrant politics in their community. Moreover, Patchogue residents, with the assistance of the New York Division of Human Rights, formed the Unity Coalition to help quell racial tensions in their community. Finally, the grassroots organization Farmingdale Citizens for Viable Solutions, along with Catholic Charities and the Workplace Project, established *La Casa Comunal* as a community center for day laborers. The citizens' group also documents hate crimes. Similarly, the Workplace Project, until recently under the leadership of Colombian-American lawyer Nadia Marin-Molina, has been the most vocal supporter of immigrant rights on Long Island and has consistently lobbied for the construction of day-labor or worker centers to formalize hiring processes and protect workers' rights.

In the last three years, Long Island advocates, concerned citizens, and immigrants – undocumented and documented – have blazed a pathway for social justice that those in similar predicaments had successfully traveled before. The immigrants' rights marches in March 2006 were a clear indication not only of the organizational strength that immigrants and their allies had harnessed over the last 25 years, but also that legislative attempts to criminalize immigrants, their families, and their supporters would not go unchecked. The Sensenbrenner Bill, commonly known as HR 4437, propelled millions of supporters of immigrant rights to publicly and collectively voice their objections against the pending legislation. James Sensenbrenner, a Republican congressman from Wisconsin, sponsored the bill that, among many questionable aims, proposed to change undocumented status in the United States from a misdemeanor civil offense to a felony crime. While HR 4437 increased the penalty for employers who hired an undocumented worker to $7,500, it also aimed to criminalize any person who in any way aided undocumented immigrants with up to five years in prison. Furthermore, the Sensenbrenner Bill called for the immediate expulsion of apprehended immigrants; in effect, denying them due process under the law. When the House of Representatives passed the Sensenbrenner Bill by a vote of 239 to 182 in late 2005, public dialogue and outcry were sparked on both sides of the immigration debate.

Instead of remaining voiceless and invisible, immigrants and their supporters countered the Sensenbrenner Bill with nationwide protests and cries of *"Hoy marchamos, manana votamos"* (Today we march, tomorrow we vote).[4] Millions of protestors participated in *La Gran Marcha* over three successive months of spring 2006. The protests against HR 4437 began in earnest in Chicago in mid-March with an estimated 500,000 immigrants and their allies rallying in support of immigrant rights and comprehensive immigration reform. Two weeks later, on March 25 and 26, protests across the nation continued, and like the earlier march in Chicago, they were comprised of a multiplicity of immigrants from Mexico, Central and South America, Asia, Africa, and the Caribbean, immigrant rights groups, students, and workers of all ethnicities, as well as some academics. Marches against the Sensenbrenner Bill were most dramatically represented by approximately 1 million people who took to the streets in Los Angeles and over 50,000 people in downtown Denver on March 25. The next day, approximately 20,000 protestors filled the streets in Phoenix and on Thursday, March 30, more than 10,000 marchers voiced their support in Milwaukee. Two weeks later, from April 10 to 11, demonstrations brought out 50,000 people in Atlanta, 500,000 in Dallas, 50,000 in San Diego, and 20,000 in Salt Lake City. College towns such as Champaign and Madison, together, turned out thousands of protestors, while Kansas meatpacking towns such as Garden City, Dodge City, and Schuler turned out a large number of protestors at high rates compared to their population: Garden City had 3,000 protestors in a city of 30,000 and Dodge City and Schuler had their meatpacking plants closed down because of worker attendance at the rally.

Protests against HR 4437 continued into early May with "A Day Without an Immigrant/Great American Boycott" rallies. Many immigrant-serving companies closed in solidarity with these protests; meatpacking plants were most affected by the boycott, but it does not appear that the consumer boycott was as large as anticipated. The Los Angeles protests continued to be the most widely supported. Latino students walked out of middle and high schools in protest of the Sensenbrenner Bill and to join immigrant supporters in a daytime and an evening rally that, according to the Spanish-language media source Univision, drew close to 2 million people. Rallies exceeding 10,000 participants were held in Seattle, Salem (OR), San José, Santa Ana, Philadelphia, Providence (RI), Orlando, Portland (OR), New York City, Chicago, Milwaukee, Denver, Atlanta, and Las Vegas. All totaled, the rallies brought out close to 5 million protestors across the nation.[5]

Protests against the Sensenbrenner Bill signaled to the American public in general and to nativist politicians in particular that nativist solutions to the so-called immigration problem would be directly challenged by immigrants and their supporters. There were some political consequences from the immigrant rallies. Republicans affiliated with the Immigration Reform Caucus, for example, lost nine seats in the House of Representatives; and politicians, at least in the short term, began looking for other types of solutions to the immigration dilemma – alternatives that were comprehensive because they sought to address a range of needs that are in keeping with a civil and human rights approach. Calls for comprehensive immigration reform led the late Senator Edward "Ted" Kennedy (Massachusetts) and Senator John McCain (Arizona) in 2007 to revive an earlier proposal that sought to create a path to legal residency for approximately 11–12 million undocumented persons that currently live and work in the United States. A guest worker program was also proposed. In late 2007, amid national debate and opposition from nativist forces and conservative talk-show hosts, the Kennedy–McCain Bill failed.

Currently, there is no legislative solution to undocumented immigration in the United States. Undocumented immigrants have no means to obtain legalization either by applying for permanent legal residency or citizenship through naturalization. This means that 11–12 million people in the United States are living in a state of illegality, which makes them not only especially vulnerable to exploitation at the workplace, but subject to immediate expulsion through raids, police stops, or other types of routine investigation. Various proposals from temporary worker programs, amnesty (a pathway toward legalization of undocumented immigrants), to mass deportations, the DREAM Act (Development, Relief, and Education for Alien Minors), workplace raids, and further criminalization comprise the range of options on immigration reform. The overall approach to immigration reform, however, is to view Latinos, irrespective of national origins or citizenship status, as the main cause of the immigration problem that if left unfettered will threaten national security, promote unfair labor competition, and burden taxpayers. Frequently, proponents of nativism express their anxieties about the future of the United States in racialized and anti-immigrant terms. The basis of such fears stems from the rapid growth in the Latino population that for the most part is attributable to high rates of immigration from Latin America. In 2008, Latinos – documented and undocumented – represented 15.1 percent of the total US population. At 43 million, they are the largest ethnic minority group in the United States, surpassing African Americans. According to Census 2010 enumerations, 16.3 percent (or 50,477,594) of the US population are Latino but current figures do not separate the foreign-born by Latino ethnicity. By March 2009, the 8.9 million undocumented immigrants from Latin America comprised the majority of the total number of undocumented immigrants (11.1 million) in the United States. Among the undocumented population, Mexicans made up the majority of unauthorized immigrants at 6.7 million (Torras and Skinner 2010). If this rate of growth continues, demographers contend, the Latino population will make up 30 percent of the total US population by 2050; whites will no longer constitute an outright majority. Likewise, should undocumented immigration continue at the same pace as that established, the vast majority of illegal immigrants will continue originating from Latin America and Mexico in particular.

The themes presented in this book are intended to underscore the complexities of Latino immigration in the United States. Of critical importance is the fact that Latino immigrants have reacted to anti-immigrant sentiment and virulent nativism in proactive ways, responding with various legal, cultural, and economic demonstrations of political influence and power. To highlight these processes, *Latino Immigrants in the United States* adopts a comparative and intra-ethnic approach to the study of Latino immigration. It demonstrates that Puerto Ricans, Dominicans, Mexicans, Chicanos, Cubans, and South and Central Americans not only have resided and worked in close proximity to one another, but that they organize politically for collective social betterment. We highlight several key instances when Mexican and Dominican immigrants have challenged nativism with the assistance of Puerto Rican, Mexican American, and Central American activists and organizations. These intra-ethnic alliances, we argue, form the bases of *Latinidad*, or "a shared sense of a Latino identity" (Rúa 2006), that unites individuals and groups, despite differences in national origins, citizenship status, and culture. This approach to Latino immigration and identity is further supported by a critical analysis of the social construction and subsequent categorization of "Latinos" and "Hispanics" by the US Census Bureau. We question the origins of these categories while emphasizing both shared aspects of *Latinidad* and the distinct points where Latino communities diverge from one another. In so doing, we offer a more complete account of the contradictions and promises of obtaining US citizenship, the impact of immigrant labor struggles in an era of neoliberalism, and the manner in which Latino immigrants have responded to restrictionist legislation and nativism. In chapter 2, "*Latinidades*: The Making of Identity and Community," the political bases for Latino experiences are highlighted and further explored as elements of a shared cultural identity: bilingualism, education, US foreign policy, nativism, immigration law, and labor organizing. This approach embeds *Latinidad* in actual lived relations. Thus, we discuss the longstanding Cuban, Puerto Rican, and Mexican destinations in the United States in relation to new Latino destinations and emerging Latino communities. Local anti-immigrant ordinances are currently framing immigration as primarily a problem of Mexicans illegally crossing the border. Interestingly, when anti-immigrant legislation was challenged in Hazleton, Pennsylvania, it was LatinoJustice/ Puerto Rican Legal Defense and Education Fund (PRLDEF) that filed the successful suit. Understanding Latinos as sharing similar racialized predicaments is crucial in understanding why a legal organization representing US citizens of Puerto Rican descent views the anti-immigrant movement as a challenge to Puerto Rican citizens in Hazleton as much as it is for Mexican, Dominican, and Central American undocumented immigrants.

Chapter 3, "Pathways to Citizenship," discusses Latino immigration along the continuum of citizenship, naturalization, and refugee/asylee statuses. It begins by tracing the politics of citizenship among Mexicans and Puerto Ricans to the nineteenth-century incorporation of Mexicans and Puerto Ricans into the United States as a means to understand how US citizenship produced various second-class statuses and categories of alienage. Puerto Ricans experience a limited form of political membership, and despite living in a supposedly self-determining territory, lack representation in the federal government and are excluded from voting in presidential elections. Likewise cession of half of Mexico to the United States in 1848 produced new distinctions between US subjects (incorporated Mexicans or Chicanos) and Mexicans south of the newly delineated border. Lastly, we examine Salvadorans and struggles for Temporary Protected Status (TPS) as well as the Cuban Adjustment Act in 1966 and its modification to the "wet feet/dry feet policy" in the 1990s.

Chapter 4, "Cultural Citizenship, Gender, and Labor," examines themes of cultural citizenship, gender relations, and labor/community organizing. In response to neo-nativism and labor exploitation, Latino immigrants are creating a space of substantive inclusion by participating in the Latino immigrant union movement and the burgeoning immigrant rights movement. In particular, Latina immigrants – Guatemalan, Salvadoran, Mexican, Cuban – have engaged in labor activism that has changed their relationship to their work, communities, and families. An exploration into the organizing efforts in Justice for Janitors (Service Employees International Union [SEIU]) and UNITE-HERE shows that Latina immigrants gain greater personal autonomy and independence as they participate in the labor force and in labor activism. As a result, long-held gender ideals and traditional household patterns are being re-evaluated and new relationships emerging that are often more egalitarian.

Chapter 5, "Transnational Identities," analyzes how Latino immigrants navigate the contemporary climate of US reception in the formation of transnational social identities. We examine how the sociological literature on Latino immigrant communities relates to assimilation, neo-nativism, racializations, transnationalism, and social identities. Dominicans are viewed as the consummate example of "transnational villagers," yet recent research on Mixtec Mexicans, Cubans, and Puerto Ricans informs how Latino transnational identities are also experienced and conceptualized. We discuss transnationalism within the context of US border militarization, the rise of nativist vigilante groups, recent deportation sweeps, local anti-immigrant legislation, and comprehensive federal immigration reform. For Latinos, the dilemmas of immigrant identity are necessarily complicated by the processes of racialization in both the United States and Latin America. Sociologists have moved beyond the assimilation/cultural pluralism debates to consider how social identities are both imposed from above (racialization and nativism) and constructed as transnational identities from below. We discuss the specific relations of Afro-Latinos from the Caribbean, and the "racing" of Mexican immigrants in this era of neoliberal nativism.

In chapter 6, "Neoliberalism and Globalization," we introduce a set of comparisons to capture the emerging migration streams from Latin America to the United States as a result of

US–Latin American free trade agreements, neoliberal reforms in Latin America, and the forces of globalization. We differentiate between globalization from above and below to identify how neoliberalism and the 1965 Employee Skills Provision led to a rise of "preference" class migration from South America (particularly Argentina, Colombia, Venezuela, Ecuador, and Peru). We also discuss the globalization-from-below survival responses to NAFTA/DR-CAFTA and how structural adjustment/neoliberal intrusions into indigenous communities in southern Mexico and Guatemala are leading to new migration streams as a direct result of export-led displacement.

Bringing the book to a close, chapter 7, "*Fronteras Nuevas/ New Frontiers,*" identifies the most pressing social issues facing Latinos in the next 25 years. If demographic projections prove accurate, Latinos will surpass whites as the majority population in the American Southwest and will represent majority populations elsewhere in the United States. We distill the bigger picture of what demographic changes mean for political, social, and economic change. Topics include demographic projections, linguistic practices, generation differences, inter-racial relations, popular culture (music, sports, film, and television), food and diet, education, housing, healthcare, demography, religion, crime, entrepreneurship, federal immigration reform, and environmental justice.

Latino Immigrants in the United States sheds light on the present-day status of a deeply misunderstood and often maligned group of people living and working in the United States, frequently at the margins of society. No longer can the US public condone an unjust and often deadly policy regarding migration from Latin America to the United States. Immigration to the United States not only has separated family and friends from one another, it has also deprived Latin America of some of its most resourceful, working-age citizens. Furthermore, it obliges border-crossers to take considerable risks to emigrate and reach their destination, and that danger hardly ceases upon arrival. Once in the United States, immigrants face exploitation, abuse, and violence. By examining Latino immigration from both sending and receiving nations – that is, from within and without the United States – and from an intra-ethnic perspective is to address the subject with a balance and thoroughness that may ultimately provide greater understanding about a social issue that promises to grow in both scope and implication.

2

Latinidades: *The Making of Identity and Community*

US circuit courts have consistently ruled that immigration enforcement is a matter of federal jurisdiction. Yet, local and state legislation aimed at enforcing immigration matters from Farmers Branch, Texas and Prince William County, Virginia to the states of Georgia and Arizona is being challenged in the courts by coalitions of Puerto Rican, Mexican, Dominican, and pan-Latino organizations. On their face, localities claim they are forcing the jurisdictional question by passing laws and ordinances that restrict immigrants' access to jobs and homes via employer sanctions, residential requirements, and deportations. Nowhere is this drama unfolding more clearly than in the small city of Hazleton at the foot of the Pennsylvanian Poconos Mountains. Listening to the mayor, one would think the city is under siege by Latino immigrants, who he characterizes as the source of social problems from increased crime to overcrowded schools. This former anthracite mining community was the site of similar nativist sentiments at the turn of the last century when the local elite characterized the increasing presence of Italians, Irish, Poles, Germans, and Greeks as an invasion. Former Hazleton mayor Italian American Lou Barletta bemoans the hordes of Latino immigrants invading the town and a wide array of Latinos are banding together to challenge their vilification, and in the process, embodying the concept of what it means to be Latino.

In 2006, the Hazleton city council passed the Illegal Immigrant Relief Act (IIRA) – an ironic title given that such immigrants were hardly intended to be recipients of good will. The ordinance (Haz-1) targeted employers and landlords who respectively hired or leased properties to undocumented immigrants. The "Relief" was directed toward citizen-residents and the law's intent was to create an inhospitable environment where undocumented immigrants would feel unwelcome and leave en masse. The law fined landlords who rented to undocumented immigrants and punished employers who hired undocumented workers, but additionally led to suspension of licenses and permits. This law was soon followed by the Tenant Registration ordinance that required tenants to provide proof of citizenship or lawful residency in order to register with the city and pay for an occupancy permit. The IIRA ordinance also created an "English only" policy in the provision of all government services. In some ways, the current anti-immigrant hysteria has resurfaced in response to few economic prospects for a region whose main industries long since departed, well prior to the arrival of Latino immigrants.

Yet the 1,132 Latinos residing in the city constituted only 4.7 percent of Hazleton's population in 2000, according to the US Census. The most recent data are a four-year estimate from the 2005–9 American Community Survey (ACS), which estimates that Latinos comprise 23.8 percent of the city's population (approximately 519 Mexicans, 568 Puerto Ricans, and 4,095 "other" Latinos). Examining the same ACS estimates for Luzerne County, the vast majority of "other" Latinos are from the Dominican Republic. In many ways, the unbroken thread of Hazleton's history involves the presence of immigrants often deemed unwanted and undesirable.

The vilified immigrant minorities of centuries past are now the majority: those categorized as white. According to the 2000 Census, the top five "ancestry" responses for the greater Hazleton area are: Italian – 11,341; Polish – 6,724; German – 4,791; Irish – 4,316; and Slovak – 3,706. Yet, it is precisely these immigrant groups who were viewed as not fully white and thus not fully American at the turn of the last century. In the early 1900s, Hazleton and eastern Pennsylvania were at the heart of labor struggles between the robber barons (including financiers such as

J.P. Morgan) and immigrant miners (represented by the United Mine Workers of America). Struggles reached fever-pitch in 1902 when anthracite coal miners struck for safer working conditions, better wages, fewer hours, collective bargaining rights, and an end to child labor. The ensuing battle followed a pattern of owners deploying the Pennsylvania National Guard, local police, and private detective agencies to break strikers. The sentiments of mine owners were expressed by spokesman George Baer during the 1902 strike: "They don't suffer ... They don't even speak English." What made this strike unique is that the federal government interceded and President Theodore Roosevelt created a fact-finding commission that would set the precedent for the federal government as arbiters in future labor struggles.

Similarly, federal intervention has also kept the twenty-first-century anti-immigrant legislation from being implemented. Yet, when injunctions were filed to keep the Hazleton laws from going into effect, the organization leading the effort was one that has historically represented the only Latino group that by definition are not immigrants. The Puerto Rican Legal Defense and Education Fund was formed in 1972 to advocate for and defend the civil rights of the Puerto Rican population residing in the United States. They advocate, mostly through legal challenges, for Puerto Rican voting rights and representation, educational opportunity for English-learners, integration in education and housing, and language rights in the workplace. In 2008, the organization changed its name to LatinoJustice to more accurately represent the constituencies it served as well as the changing nature of politics from group-specific to pan-Latino coalitions. The case *Lozano* v. *City of Hazleton* (2006) sought an injunction on the constitutional grounds of supremacy clause, preemption, and due process in addition to Section 1981 of the Fair Housing Act and state laws. The ruling by District Court Judge James Munley was reaffirmed by the Third Circuit US Court of Appeals. The decision is quite specific in countering the claims of the mayor and city council about immigrants as law breakers and fostering an overall hostile climate created for many Latinos, in spite of their varied citizenship statuses (a topic we turn to in the next chapter).

In this chapter, we discuss the manner in which Latino identity is both an imposed construction and how it is being re-embodied in the politics and daily experiences of similarly situated Latino immigrants.

Imposing the Hispanic Category

When thinking about how the Latino community is constituted, it is helpful to visit the Spanish derivation of the word "*Comunidad*" as the combination of *común* and *unidad*. The question becomes: what do Latinos have in "common" and what "unites" them; or, what are Latinos' commonalities that provide the fertile ground for potential forms of acting and thinking in unity? The word *común* refers to sharing those aspects in the cultures of the various constitutive groups that overlap. *Unidad* is that which binds the groups above and beyond their diverse particularities. If we conceive of Latino communities as "imagined communities" (Anderson 2006; Camacho 2008), we begin to understand both the contingent nature of solidarity and internal conflict and the necessary struggles for political alliances and coalition building within an emerging context of the increasing presence of "other" Latinos who are more often residing in new destinations.

As scholars struggle to keep pace with these profound changes, a sense of *Latinidad* can be gleaned from the shared historical connection of Latin America to Spanish colonialism and US imperialism. Additionally, upon entering the United States, an imposed Hispanic identity is thrust upon groups in official government and particularly US Census impositions of the Hispanic ethnic category. There is a convergence of Latin American Studies (post-Cold War) meeting the rise in Latino Studies out of the divergent Chicano and Puerto Rican Studies strands of nationalist civil rights. Stephen et al. (2003) describe an emerging "Las Américas" project to conceive of the interconnectedness of the Americas and particularly how Spanish colonialism and US imperialism shape the making of Latin America and a sense of *Latinidad* among Latino immigrants in the United States.

The "idea" of Latin America is that sad one of the elites celebrating their dreams of becoming modern while they slide deeper and deeper into the logic of coloniality. The idea of "Latin" America that came into view in the second half of the nineteenth century depended in varying degrees on an idea of "Latinidad" – "Latinity", "Latinitée" – that was being advanced by France. "Latinidad" was precisely the ideology under which the identity of the ex-Spanish and ex-Portuguese colonies was located (by natives as well as by Europeans) in the new global, modern/colonial world order. When the idea of "Latinidad" was launched it had a particular purpose within European impe- rial conflicts and a particular function in redrawing the imperial difference. (Mignolo 2005: 58)

The US government has long been confounded by the complexities that Latinos pose for the collection of racial and ethnic statistics. The first US collection of racial statistics distinguished between the slave population and free whites, which coincided with the 1790 Naturalization Act that limited US citizenship to white, male property owners. The nineteenth century continued this racial dualism of either white or black (the black–white binary) to characterize the population. For the first time in 1930, the Census categorized Mexicans as one of the 39 enumerated races. Though underestimated because some Mexicans were categorized as white by enumerators, the 1930 Mexican race comprised 1.2 percent, or 1,422,533, of the total US population. Often not noted is that Cubans, Spaniards, and Spanish Americans were also enumerated in 1910–30 censuses, according to the Dillingham Commission's report as summarized by Jenks and Lauck (1926: 666–9). In 1910, the US Census counted 39,562 Cubans, 5,837 Spanish, and 900 Spanish Americans. The Commission represented the zenith of anti-immigrant sentiments and eventually led to the Johnson– Reed Immigration Act of 1924, which severely restricted the flow of immigrants from Southern and Eastern Europe, by placing national quotas to minimize who and how many might enter, while completely barring immigration from Asia. The 1924 Act also created the Border Patrol, designed to further restrict entry into the United States.

The Mexican population in the United States went through

Latinidades: *The Making of Identity and Community*

Table 2.1. 1910–30 Census and Mexican Race by Nativity

Census Year	Total	Native	Foreign-Born
1930	1,422,533	805,535	616,998
1920 (estimated)	700,541	243,181	457,360
1910 (estimated)	367,510	156,277	211,233

Source: Compiled with statistics from the US Census Bureau.

dramatic growth from 1910 to 1930 in response to the violence and instability resulting from the Mexican Revolution (see table 2.1). Unlike any other immigrant group in US history, they were targeted for forced repatriation during the Great Depression, and the Hoover administration went to great lengths to scapegoat Mexican immigrants for the high levels of unemployment, hoping to deflect attention away from the stock market crash and corporate malfeasance. Estimates vary but at least 500,000 and likely more than 1 million Mexicans (immigrants, legal residents, and US citizens) were deported en masse during the Depression (including the deportation of one-third of Los Angeles' Mexican population and nearly all of Detroit's Mexican population).

Spanish-speaking, Spanish American, and Spanish-surnamed categories accounted for approximately 1.8 million Latinos in the 1940 Census. Population growth was spurred primarily by the postwar *Gran Migración* from Puerto Rico (the US-bound population expanded from 70,000 in 1940 to over 300,000 in 1950) and the direct recruitment of approximately 2 million Mexican farmworkers under the auspices of the US–Mexico Bracero Program (1942–64).[6] The category "Spanish" often became shorthand for Puerto Ricans in the Northeast and Mexicans in the Southwest. As US economic policy forced rural Puerto Ricans to flee the island, industrialization often resulted in migration first to New York City and then other cities along the eastern seaboard. Operation Bootstrap was highly effective as a policy that allowed US corporations to locate a cheap source of labor in Puerto Rico but the attempts at modernization more often resulted in increasing migration than fostering economic development. The investments were clearly one-sided in their design and while US corporations benefited from tariff-free and federal tax shelters, there rarely resulted a mass improvement in quality of life for residents of Puerto Rico. The collection of racial statistics at this time was more in terms of tracking population flows and family size to justify events such as *La Operación* in Puerto Rico, which resulted in the forced sterilization of nearly one-third of women of child-bearing age on the island.

In the pursuit of equal rights, the collection of racial statistics after 1960 was designed to determine status eligibility for civil rights protection and affirmative action participation. "Drawing on the categories employed in a 1950 government form, the Equal Employment Opportunity Commission (EEOC) in 1964 identified four minority groups: Negro, Spanish-American, American-Indian, and Asian" (Prewitt 2005: 8). Yet in the same decade, the US Census categorized all Latinos as white. "In the 1960 census, enumerators were instructed to record: Puerto Ricans, Mexicans, or other persons of Latin American descent as 'White' unless they were definitely of Negro, Indian, or other non-white race" (Bennett 2000: 172).

The discrepancy between being categorized as simultaneously a minority and part of the majority was not fixed in the decade between 1960 and 1970, even though there was a shift from imputation to self-identification. Not done for noble reasons of racial accuracy and self-clarification, in reality there were many more mail-surveys distributed in the 1970 Census (approximately 70 percent of households received mail-in questionnaires); thus, direct enumeration was next to impossible. The history, from 1790 to 1960, of enumerators determining the race of respondents was officially over.

In 1970, the questionnaires remained essentially the same as 1960 but respondents were asked to choose their race. The option was only one circle could be filled in and for Latinos, the only applicable bubble was "other" unless they self-identified as Black, White, American Indian, certain Asian national origins, or Hawaiian. It wasn't until the passage of Public Law 94-311 in 1976 that US Congress passed a law "relating to the publication of economic and social statistics for Americans of Spanish origin or descent":

> Signed by President Gerald Ford in June 1976, it remains the only law in the country's history that mandates the collection, analysis, and publication of data for a specific ethnic group, and goes on to define the population to be enumerated. The law, building on information gathered from the 1970 census, asserted that "more than twelve million Americans identify themselves as being of Spanish-speaking background and trace their origin or descent from Mexico, Puerto Rico, Cuba, Central and South America, and other Spanish-speaking countries"; that a "large number" of them "suffer from racial, social, economic, and political discrimination and are denied the basic opportunities that they deserve as American citizens"; and that an "accurate determination of the urgent and special needs of Americans of Spanish origin and descent" was needed to improve their economic and social status. (Rumbaut 2009: 23)

The resulting operationalization of this law was issued in May 1977 by the Office of Management and Budget's (OMB) Statistical Policy Directive Number 15 related to "Race and Ethnic Standards for Federal Statistics and Administrative Reporting." The directive defined a Hispanic as: "A person of Mexican, Puerto Rican, Cuban, Central or South American or other Spanish culture or origin, regardless of race." Hispanic was thus defined as an ethnic group that derives its ancestry from Spanish-speaking nations. Though Rumbaut is technically correct in stating that Public Law 94-311 was the first to mandate the collection of data for an *ethnic* group, requirements for measuring racial groups are as old as the Census itself (see figure 2.1 for the Census 2010 question format to determine US residents' ethnic and racial status).

The term "Hispanic" was coined by the US government, but has no organic resonance with the manner in which Latino communities actually identify themselves. For both Latino immigrants and US-born Latinos, the Census categories simply do not coincide with identities based on conceptualizations of race in Latin America or identities constructed via national origins. The imposed term brought together disparate groups that often lived in completely different regions and embodied distinct migration and reception histories. It also imputed specific racialized notions that Latinos defy to this day. "For the past three decades, Hispanics have been able to check Hispanic ethnicity along with 'some other race' on the census. (An unprecedented 42.2 percent of Hispanics checked 'some other race' on the 2000 census. Moreover, 97 percent of those checking 'some other race' were Hispanics). Put differently, the 'some other race' option has served as a political safety valve for the Census Bureau by masking the stark opposition that the official U.S. taxonomy mandates between ethnicity and race, and the rather inadequate race options available to Hispanics" (Hattam 2005: 66).

The Census defines race not as a scientific or anthropological categorization, but as one that categorizes people by tracing "origins" to Europe/North Africa/Middle East (white), Black Africa, Asia, Americas, or Pacific Islands (see figure 2.1). Sociologists Michael Omi and Howard Winant (1994: 55) explain: "Race is a concept that signifies and symbolizes social conflicts and interests by referring to different types of bodies, cultures, religions, or traditions. Although the concept of race invokes biologically based characteristics (so-called 'phenotypes') selection of these particular features for purposes of racial signification is always and necessarily a social and historical process." By understanding race as a social and historical construction, the latent biological and more manifest cultural or geographic origins approach certainly questions the fixity of currently deployed racial categories that slights Latino inclusion. In 2000, the US Census dropped the requirement that people self-identify as solely one race. Harkening back to longstanding essentialisms about race and the "one-drop" rule that claimed one drop of black blood confirmed a person's racial status as black, the multiracial option (checking off more than one race) ended the one-race rule. In the 2010 Census, only about 2.9 percent of the US population self-identified as more than one race. For Latino immigrants, who more often explicitly trace their origins in mixed-race terms (specifically through *mestizaje* or mixtures of Spanish, African, and indigenous heritage), the Census-imposed US racial categories simply do not make sense

8. Is Person 1 of Hispanic, Latino, or Spanish origin?

☐ **No,** not of Hispanic, Latino, or Spanish origin
☐ Yes, Mexican, Mexican Am., Chicano
☐ Yes, Puerto Rican
☐ Yes, Cuban
☐ Yes, another Hispanic, Latino, or Spanish origin — *Print origin, for example, Argentinean, Colombian, Dominican, Nicaraguan, Salvadoran, Spaniard, and so on.* ⟋

```

```

9. What is Person 1's race? *Mark* X *one or more boxes.*

☐ White
☐ Black, African Am., or Negro
☐ American Indian or Alaska Native — *Print name of enrolled or principal tribe.* ⟋

```

```

☐ Asian Indian   ☐ Japanese   ☐ Native Hawaiian
☐ Chinese   ☐ Korean   ☐ Guamanian or Chamorro
☐ Filipino   ☐ Vietnamese   ☐ Samoan
☐ Other Asian — *Print race, for*   ☐ Other Pacific Islander — *Print*
  example, Hmong, Laotian, Thai,   *race, for example, Fijian, Tongan,*
  Pakistani, Cambodian, and so on. ⟋   *and so on.* ⟋

```

```

☐ Some other race — *Print race.* ⟋

```

```

Figure 2.1   Census 2010 Race and Hispanic Ethnicity Questions

as viable options when "Hispanic" was imputed as an ethnic category, separate from one's race.

A primary complication in ascertaining the Latino population is the US's inconsistency in the application of its labels. Depending on the agency and the "long" or "short" protocols of OMB Directive 15, one finds Latinos are sometimes defined as a race. At other times, only Puerto Rican and Mexican American citizens comprise the Latino minority category for purposes of program eligibility. Directive 15, under the auspices of the OMB, gives the option to respondents of collapsing race and ethnicity questions to make Latinos one of the five options and not a separate ethnicity question. By contrast, other divisions such as the EEOC, Office of Civil Rights, and other programs that implement the Civil Rights Acts of 1964, 1965, and 1968 define Latinos as racialized groups to be protected from discrimination. In defining who Latinos are, the US Census' variable patterns of inclusion and exclusion point to a distinct lack of historical congruence between contemporary and past categorizations and current inconsistencies that obscure accurate representations of the largest minority group in the nation.

For instance, the US Census does not define Brazilians (the fourth largest immigrant group from South America behind Colombians, Ecuadorians, and Peruvians) as Hispanic due to their former status as a Portuguese colony. Their situation fully epitomizes the arbitrarily imposed label of Latino or more accurately Hispanic. Brazil traces its history to a mixture of European colonizer, indigenous colonized, and African slaves. Official Brazilian Census measures find that Black and mixed-race Brazilians utilize 125 terms to classify their "color." Many used vague terms like *criollo* (mixed ancestry) and *moreno* (dark-skinned) and even though approximately 50 percent of Brazil's 165 million people are of African descent – making it the second largest Black population behind Africa's largest nation, Nigeria – only 6 percent of the population classify themselves as Black.

Similarly, French-speaking Haiti is a nation that shares the island of Hispaniola (as Columbus dubbed it in the name of the Spanish Crown in 1492) with the Dominican Republic. Haitians are not categorized as Latinos; but Dominicans are. As a French colony turned free-slave nation, a distinct Haitian diasporic culture arose in the United States, particularly in Louisiana in the late 1800s. The movement to challenge Louisiana's Separate Car Act was launched first by the New Orleans *Comité des Citoyens*, an organization of Haitian-origin New Orleans residents. A Haitian American of light-complexion named Homere A. Plessy was chosen by the committee to break the law and sit in a railcar reserved for whites only. Their case was initially successful at the state level but when the US Supreme Court weighed in on *Plessy* v. *Ferguson*, the 1896 doctrine of "separate but equal" became the law of the nation. Ensuing Jim Crow segregation was upheld in the courts until *Brown* v. *Board of Education* in 1954. Plessy's challenge to segregation was squarely rooted in Haitians' connections to African American struggles for equality. Most people are not aware of Louisiana's Haitian diaspora and their battles for racial equality in Baltimore, New York, Philadelphia, and Charleston. At the time, the justices were well aware of the challenges posed by Haitian activism and chose to render their negative decision on May 18, 1896 – Haitian Flag Day (Laguerre 1998). That Haitians may share both a history and a contemporary reality linking them to Latinos escaped the consideration of a US Census Bureau that categorizes Haitians solely as African Americans.

The Bureau's criteria for inclusion versus exclusion as "Hispanic" (geographic origin, language, prior Spanish colonial status, ethnicity but not race) make it difficult to understand how Argentinians are considered Latino but Filipinos are not; why Costa Ricans are Latino but Belizeans are not; why Spaniards are Latino but Cape Verdeans are not; why Cubans and Puerto Ricans are Latino but peoples of the Caribbean islands of the West Indies are not; why Dominicans from the Dominican Republic are Latino but Dominicans from Dominica are not. This imposed ethnic category and its numerous limitations cut to the heart of identity formation: are identities imposed from outside agents or constructed by individuals themselves? Are they essentialist and unchanging, or additive and developmental; unitary or multiple; mutually exclusive or intersecting and overlapping? For Latinos, these questions become the basis for shared conversations about how the category of Latino is embodied in daily lived experiences. For Latino immigrants, understanding what it means to be Latino is informed both from their nation of origin and the communities they migrate to within the United States.

Latino Destinations: Aztlán, Nuyorican El Barrio, and Little Havana

Analyses by Diaz-McConnell (2003) and Diaz-McConnell and Guzmán (2003) demonstrate that US Census, American Community Survey (ACS), and Current Population Survey (CPS) estimates of the Latino population tend to vary so significantly that accurate and reliable numbers are often difficult to come by. Recent CPS estimates of the Latino population in the United States put the number at close to 46.9 million in 2008 (51 million if Puerto Rico is included), while the ACS estimated the Latino population in 2008 to be 45.4 million (or 49.3 million including Puerto Rico). Either estimate is a significant increase from the findings of the 2000 Census, which identified 35.2 million Latinos in the United States (or 39.0 million if Puerto Rico is included). The Latino population is clearly increasing as the 2010 Census identifies 50,477,594 Latinos residing in the United States (54,166,049 with Puerto Rico included). The largest Latino national origins groups in 2000 were: Mexicans (20.9 million); Puerto Ricans (3.4 million; 7.2 million if residents of the island itself are included); Cubans (1.2 million); Dominicans (800,000); and Salvadorans (800,000). At that time, Latinos lived in nearly every county of the United States but are concentrated in the counties and states along the US–Mexico border, South Florida, and rural regions such as eastern Washington State (see figure 2.2).

As previously noted, the Latino population within the United States has continued to grow dramatically, although the prevalence of its various subgroups has tended to remain fairly constant. In 2008, the ACS broke down the Latino subgroup as follows: Mexican (29.3 million); Puerto Rican (4.1 million; 7.9 million including residents of the island); Cuban (1.6 million); Salvadoran (1.5 million); and Dominican (1.2 million). These estimates indicate that most counties in California, the New York–Boston corridor, Chicago, Florida, Texas, and Nevada, as well as several rural counties in Georgia, North Carolina, Michigan, Oregon, and

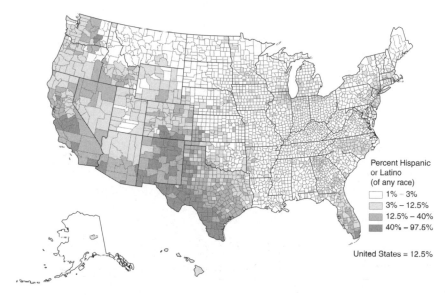

Figure 2.2 Latino Population by County Concentration, 2000

Source: Adapted from US Census Bureau (Census of Population and Housing), 2000

Washington State and the front range of Colorado all have more than 50,000 Latino residents.

The Latino rank order by national origin is identified in table 2.2. The limitations of the US Census categories are apparent in its inability to accurately account for 5.2 percent of the Latino population that self-designate as "all other Spanish/Hispanic/Latino." This miscellany group is larger than all but the Mexican and Puerto Rican populations. The confusion is exacerbated by the fact that at times the population includes the island of Puerto Rico and at other times it does not. There are also clear variations among the percent foreign-born and national origins Latino groups. Though Mexicans are the vast majority of immigrants, only 37 percent of Mexicans are foreign-born. The Latin American nations that started seeing their populations move northward after the 1965 Immigration and Nationality Act (INA) have much higher percentages of foreign-born residents. Nations most directly targeted

Table 2.2. Latinos by National Origin and Foreign-Born Status, 2008

	US States	Puerto Rico	Combined States and Puerto Rico	Percent of Latinos	Percent Foreign-Born (Top Ten)
Total Population	301,237,703	3,940,626	305,178,329	—	12.4
Total Latino Population	45,420,992	3,893,042	49,314,034	100.0	38.1
1. Mexican	29,354,305	11,190	29,365,495	59.5	37.0
2. Puerto Rican	4,104,979	3,762,593	7,867,572	16.0	1.1
3. Cuban	1,576,028	19,172	1,595,200	3.2	60.1
4. Salvadoran	1,461,782	662	1,462,444	3.0	64.7
5. Dominican	1,248,424	68,681	1,317,105	2.7	57.3
6. Guatemalan	917,503	601	918,104	1.9	69.4
7. Colombian	812,864	4,062	825,926	1.7	66.5
8. Honduran	540,297	449	540,746	1.1	68.6
9. Ecuadorian	531,361	988	532,349	1.1	66.4
10. Peruvian	469,824	1,199	471,023	1.0	69.3
11. Spaniard	453,956	4,504	458,460	0.9	—
12. Nicaraguan	317,948	811	318,759	0.6	—
13. Argentinian	192,262	1,720	193,982	0.4	—
14. Venezuelan	187,155	2,643	189,798	0.4	—
15. Panamanian	140,361	1,402	141,763	0.3	—
16. Costa Rican	115,806	283	116,089	0.2	—
17. Chilean	111,696	768	112,464	0.2	—
18. Bolivian	87,755	484	88,239	0.2	—

19. Uruguayan	52,723	298	53,021	0.1	—
20. Paraguayan	17,950	0	17,950	0.0	—
Other Central American	90,815	26	90,841	0.2	—
Other South American	56,743	65	56,808	0.1	—
All Other Spanish/ Hispanic/Latino	2,569,455	10,441	2,579,896	5.2	—

Source: US Census Bureau, American Community Survey. Adapted from National Institute for Latino Policy (NiLP) and Pew Hispanic Center.

by US imperialism and Cold War foreign policies have the highest rates of foreign-born residing in the United States.

By the end of the twenty-first century, if the Latino population continues to increase at the same proportional level, they may comprise the outright majority group in the US population. Century-long predictions are often bad guesses but slightly more probable 50-year estimates by the Pew Hispanic Center and US Census tend to place the future Latino population at approximately 130 million (more than double its current size). If that continues to the century's end, Latinos would surpass the 44 percent share of the estimated 2050 white population. Those same estimates identify 2038 as the year when the racial majority will become the numerical minority in the United States (see Passel and Cohn 2008; Ortman and Guarnieri 2009).

Up until 2000, the prevailing wisdom in both scholarly and popular accounts held that the Latino category was comprised of Mexicans residing in the Southwest, Cubans in south Florida, and Puerto Ricans in New York City. The most influential scholarly books of the time – Massey et al. (1987), Acuña (1988), Griswold del Castillo and De León (1996), Montejano (1987), Portes and Bach (1985), Portes and Stepick (1993), García (1996), and Sánchez-Korrol (1994) – were crucial in connecting Mexicans, Cubans, and Puerto Ricans to their respective traditional destinations.

The major focus of Chicano (Mexican American) history was until quite recently centered on the communities that predated the US occupation of northern Mexico or what became after 1848 the American Southwest. Rarely a story of migration, this first wave of research told the story of US nation building and imperialism. The community studies approach to longstanding Mexican American cities such as San Antonio, East Los Angeles, Santa Barbara, Tucson, El Paso, and the south Texas region defined Chicano Studies until later waves of migration were seriously considered. Scholars such as Rudy Acuña, Juan Gomez-Quiñones, Richard Griswold del Castillo, and Arnoldo De León exemplified the Chicano Movement-era characterization of the US Southwest as an occupied territory: a land stolen by the United States as colonizer in a region defined as the original homelands of the Mexican people (*Aztlán* in Mexica/Aztec creation stories).

Sociologists of Mexican migration tended to ignore this long history of disenfranchisement and most often conducted survey research to document the present size, distribution, and human and social capital outcomes of Mexico's most recent sojourners (an important recent exception is Telles and Ortiz 2008). Surveys by Portes and Bach (1985) and Doug Massey's Mexican Migration Project (MMP) sought to provide nationally representative samples of Mexican immigrants but each were limited in some way; for example, Massey's MMP focused on Mexican immigrants residing in Houston. Portes and Bach were interested in empirically testing the proposition that Mexicans are economic migrants while Cubans can be understood as political migrants, but they too identify (and draw their sample from) the urban Southwest as the main recipient of Mexican immigrants.

Extending the analysis of Cubans as refugees or political migrants, Portes (with Bach and Stepick) describes how Miami became the quintessential ethnic enclave. The enclave was premised upon "first, a stable market that small firms can control by offering to the immigrant community culturally defined goods and services not available on the outside; second, privileged access to a pool of cheap labor through networks within the community; and third, access to capital" (Portes and Stepick 1993: 127). Little Havana, as detailed by Portes and his colleagues, is comprised of high social solidarity bonds, high levels of social and human capital, high rates of ethnic entrepreneurship, and generally high rates of upward mobility.

With the subsequent second and third waves of Cuban refugees, it became apparent that the importance of federal government financial support and subsidies had been understated by Portes and his colleagues. The resultant class and racial cleavages between the first wave and the rest clearly showed the holes in the ethnic enclave argument. García (1996) offers a nuanced, historically informed analysis of the three waves of Cuban refugees and notes that the subsequent waves of working-class Afro-Cubans questioned the automatic social mobility of the enclave. "Emigrés of the first wave (1959–1962), disproportionately white and middle class, will find it difficult to relate to the new immigrants, whom they consider rough, poor and uneducated. The fact that many of the new immigrants are black or of mixed racial heritage, and were once the faithful revolutionary proletariat, widens the cultural chasm" (García 1996: xi). She observes that third wave Marielitos (referring to the Mariel Boatlift) and fourth wave *balseros* (a derisive term used to refer to Afro-Latino Cubans) in particular found a very different reception upon arrival than the first-generation Cubans who were welcomed with open arms and the open pocketbooks of the US government. The larger migration patterns followed four very discernible stages where race relations in Cuba became mapped onto the US color line. The first to leave during the Revolution were the big business owners, hotel and tourism managers, government leaders, wealthy landowners, and other elite that were not sympathetic to communism. Miami became the major recipient but other cities played host to this group with high levels of economic and social capital. Following the elite, the middle class (teachers, professionals, managers) who did not want to live under Castro also left and settled in Little Havana, Miami, and nearby Hialeah.

The racial hierarchy of Cuba does not differ significantly from other Spanish Caribbean nations. White or Europeans were the elite, followed by a *mestizo* or *criollo* middle class, and lastly a predominately African working class. With the Mariel Boatlift in 1980 and the subsequent presence of Afro-Latino Cubans in Miami, the old racial and class order of Cuba now had a new home in south Florida.

New York's Spanish Harlem, *El Barrio*, is most often evoked as emblematic of Puerto Ricans' cultural experiences in the United States. Sánchez-Korrol's (1994: 46–7) definitive history of Puerto Ricans in New York City identifies that migrants "came on the steamship shuttles between San Juan and New York, ignoring closer destinations because New York represented familiarity and better resources. In time, they came by air, becoming the first airborne migration in history. And when they came, particularly to New York City, they formed communities and settlements frequently reflecting those left behind." The majority of early scholars in Puerto Rican Studies acknowledged migration streams to Chicago, Philadelphia, and other Northeast destinations but the main focus was *El Barrio*, where a burgeoning *Nuyorican* (Puerto Ricans who were born and raised predominately in New York City) political and cultural movement epitomized the end point of Puerto Rico's *Gran Migración*. Whalen (2001: 2) notes that "Although scholarly and public attention has focused on New York City, the history of Puerto Rican migration has been defined by dispersion. Whereas 88 percent of US Puerto Ricans lived in New York City in 1940, only 58 percent made the city their home in 1970." In 2008, only 19 percent of Puerto Ricans living in the United States called New York City home.

Yet recent data suggest a certain degree of residual accuracy with regard to the ultimate destinations of Latino immigrants. For example, approximately 70 percent of all US-based Mexicans reside in the four border states of California, Texas, New Mexico, and Arizona (table 2.3). Moreover, Mexicans constitute between 26 and 30 percent of the total population in each of the states.

In many ways, the major urban centers of the four states are clear harbingers of the national demographic shifts to come. Los Angeles, Houston, Phoenix, Albuquerque, and San Antonio are all major destinations for Mexican immigrants. Latinos constitute from 42 to 61 percent of each city's total population (table 2.4). Los Angeles is home to more Mexicans than nearly any other city in the world, second only to Mexico City. Mexicans comprise the vast majority of Latinos residing in the urban Southwest and are quickly becoming the majority group in each of the major urban centers of the Southwest.

ACS data for 2008 on Miami-Dade County (US Census Bureau 2009) revealed that Latinos represent the outright majority of the county's population (close to two-thirds of the total population) and Cubans represent nearly one-third of all county residents (table 2.5). Similar to Mexicans in Los Angeles, Miami is home to the largest Cuban population in the world outside Cuba's capital city of Havana. Interestingly, Miami, an increasingly global city, has emerged as the capital for commerce and trade in

Table 2.3. Latinos in the Southwest by State, 2008

	California		Texas		New Mexico		Arizona	
	Total	%	Total	%	Total	%	Total	%
Total Population	36,418,499	100	23,845,989	100	1,962,226	100	6,343,952	100
Latino	13,160,978	36.1	8,566,395	35.9	873,171	44.5	1,877,267	29.6
Mexican	10,945,390	30.1	7,310,195	30.7	483,759	24.7	1,681,834	26.5
Puerto Rican	165,786	0.5	104,564	0.4	7,595	0.4	30,287	0.5
Cuban	81,443	0.2	37,930	0.2	3,582	0.2	8,913	0.1
Other Latino	1,968,359	5.4	1,113,706	4.7	378,235	19.3	156,233	2.5
Dominican	8,907	0.0	10,514	0.0	604	0.0	2,292	0.0
Central American	1,108,917	3.0	391,144	1.6	6,202	0.3	38,109	0.6
South American	277,798	0.8	120,941	0.5	4,297	0.2	22,124	0.3

Source: Adapted from US Census Bureau American Fact Finder data.

Table 2.4. Major Urban Recipients of Latinos, 2008

	Los Angeles County		Houston		San Antonio		Albuquerque		Phoenix	
	Total	%	Total	%	Total	%	Total	%	Total	%
Total Population	9,832,127	100	2,024,379	100	1,227,322	100	507,823	100	1,468,633	100
Latino	4,652,748	47.3	849,226	41.9	782,220	61.2	223,455	44.0	617,968	42.1
Mexican	3,583,381	36.4	644,867	31.9	659,461	51.6	103,304	20.3	563,747	38.4
Puerto Rican	43,489	0.4	7,220	0.4	11,101	0.9	3,117	0.6	7,573	0.5
Cuban	39,991	0.4	6,013	0.3	2,074	0.2	2,308	0.5	2,999	0.2
Other Latino	985,887	10.0	191,126	9.4	109,584	8.6	114,726	22.6	43,649	3.0

Source: Adapted from US Census Bureau American Fact Finder data.

Table 2.5. Latinos in Miami-Dade, Florida, New York City, and New York, 2008

	Miami-Dade County		State of Florida		New York City		State of New York	
	Total	%	Total	%	Total	%	Total	%
Total Population	2,385,876	100	18,182,321	100	8,308,163	100	19,428,881	100
Latino	1,472,731	61.7	3,725,173	20.5	2,287,905	27.5	3,194,111	16.5
Mexican	44,913	1.9	575,745	3.2	282,965	3.4	399,237	2.1
Puerto Rican	89,458	3.7	714,153	3.9	784,065	9.4	1,084,417	5.6
Cuban	777,486	32.6	1,080,472	5.9	42,209	0.5	69,420	0.4
Other Latino	560,874	23.5	1,354,803	7.5	1,178,666	14.2	1,641,037	8.4
Dominican			142,586	0.8			656,093	3.4
Central American			408,668	2.2			309,241	1.6
South American			604,021	3.3			512,820	2.6

Source: Adapted from US Census Bureau American Fact Finder data.

Latin America and the Caribbean. Only 18 percent of the county's population self-designate as non-Hispanic white (the exact same percentage as the African American population). Sizable influxes of Haitians (who found themselves completely castigated by all racial groups in Miami) and Nicaraguans (following the enclave model of incorporation due to their co-ethnic and ideological resonance with the Cuban elite) helped to create a multicultural Miami that was more heavily characterized by social division and racial inequality. "The Nicaraguan exodus, like the Cuban, converged in successive stages on Miami, beginning with the elites, then incorporating the professional and middle classes, and lastly the working class" (Portes and Stepick 1993: 150). Consequently, the intra-ethnic divisions along class lines are often placed on the very complicated racialized spaces of a hyper-segregated city.

In New York City, the percentage of "other Latinos" – as the Census designates all Latinos not from Mexico, Cuba, or Puerto Rico – is currently outpacing the Puerto Rican population. For instance, Dominicans in Washington Heights, Colombians and Ecuadorians in Corona-Queens, and Mexicans throughout the city (including *El Barrio*) are complicating the longstanding characterization of *Nuyorican* predominance. Recognizing that Latinos comprise nearly 30 percent of the city's population (table 2.5), their presence within a city that is 25 percent African American and 12 percent Asian signals both the processes of white flight that saw millions of European immigrant descendants flee to the suburbs and a rate of in-migration that marks global cities as major immigrant destinations for years to come.

Latino, USA

The current state of sociological research on Latino immigrant destinations is less and less focused on Cubans in Florida, Puerto Ricans in New York City, and Mexicans in the US Southwest. What sociologists now identify is the increasing presence of new destinations and new Latino immigrants in the reshaping of multiple communities across the entire United States.

The emergent sociological literature on "new" destinations identifies that Latino immigrants are no longer settling exclusively in established destinations and that new migrant streams are depositing immigrants in suburban and rural localities that previously had not received Latino immigrants in large numbers (see Zúñiga and Hernández-León 2006; Massey 2008). "Puerto Ricans are no longer the majority among Hispanics in New York, nor are Cubans the majority among Latinos in Florida. Each is still the single-largest national-origin group in these states, but each is also outnumbered by the combined Other Latinos" (Jones-Correa 2007: 23). These trends, though slowing as a result of the financial downturn, are clearly not receding and immigrants are making these destinations their long-term residences.

The most recent research on new destinations has identified that Latinos are the largest minority group in the United States and there is a rapidly increasing in-migration to non-traditional receiving areas such as new non-metropolitan immigrant gateways (Massey 2008; Singer et al. 2008). In particular, a rapid in-migration of Latinos to rural regions that would otherwise be experiencing a decline in total population has become a recent demographic trend that scholars are only beginning to uncover (see Millard and Chapa 2004; Mize et al. 2009). Chicago has long been both a Puerto Rican and Mexican destination. New York City, a longstanding Puerto Rican destination, is now home to hundreds of thousands of Ecuadorians, Colombians, Mexicans, and Dominicans. The southern United States is experiencing the highest rate of growth and every Latino national origin group is contributing to this rapid population increase. *Latinidad* emerges when these groups find themselves sharing the same spaces, utilizing the same public institutions, and in the process of daily interaction creating a sense of what it means to be "Latino." Scholarly work came to reflect this shared notion of *Latinidad*; in the process of expanding the geographical scope, so we turn first to the longstanding Puerto Rican and Mexican destination of Chicago, Illinois.

The city of Chicago is currently home to well over 750,000 Latinos (table 2.6). Since the early 1900s, the city has served as a major Mexican destination or residential area as meatpacking plants and steel mills drew Mexicans away from work on the railroads. Chicago was the second largest recipient of Puerto Ricans during the *Gran Migración* and though most Puerto Ricans settled on the near northwest side and Mexicans settled on the south side, an emergent Latino identity first identified by Padilla (1985) has catalyzed the imposed Latino category into a similar panethnic consciousness and often a shared lived reality. More recent ethnographic research in the city points to bifurcated communities, defined less by a shared sense of Latino identity than by national origin (see Arredondo 2008; De Genova 2005; De Genova and Ramos-Zayas 2003; Pérez 2004; Ramos-Zayas 2003). Specifically, De Genova and Ramos-Zayas analyze the intra-Latino racializations in Chicago. "Mexican migrants often generalized from the allegation that Puerto Ricans were 'lazy' to posit variously that they were likewise untrustworthy, deceptive, willing to cheat, disagreeable, nervous, rude, aggressive, violent, dangerous, and criminal. In constructing these racialized images of the character of Puerto Ricans as a group, Mexicans were implicitly or explicitly celebrating a sense of themselves as educated, well-mannered, and civilized" (De Genova and Ramos-Zayas 2003: 83). Unfortunately, these mutual racializations or stereotypes did not originate in Mexican interactions with Puerto Ricans and are more akin to longstanding Anglo surface representations of Latinos that can trace their origins to Oscar Lewis' culture of poverty thesis that was applied to both Mexican and Puerto Rican communities. What is lost in the focus on intra-Latino racializations, particularly as Mexicans came to predominate even in Puerto Rican Chicago, is how a shared project of *Latinidad*, in opposition to Anglo racism, is increasingly defining city politics in an era of a burgeoning immigrant rights movement, a resurgence in labor organizing, and a major dispersion of Latinos beyond their traditional neighborhoods, in defiance of Chicago's longstanding practice of residential hyper-segregation.

One cannot minimize the role that racial segregation plays in the maintenance of Mexican and Latino neighborhoods. For

Table 2.6. Latinos in Chicago City, 2008

	Total	%
Total Population	2,725,206	100
Latino	758,877	27.8
Mexican	558,125	20.5
Puerto Rican	101,890	3.7
Cuban	7,509	0.3
Other Latino	91,353	3.4

Source: Adapted from US Census Bureau American Fact Finder data.

years, South Chicago's Little Village (*La Villita*) was viewed, alongside Pilsen, as the Mexican heart of Chicago:

> Long considered to be the most important "port of entry" neighborhood for newly arrived Mexican migrants, the Near West Side (Hull House) neighborhood, where Mexican migrants first settled because of its proximity to railroad yards, was ultimately decimated by "urban renewal" projects associated with the construction of expressways and the University of Illinois' Chicago campus during the 1950s and 1960s. . . . Much of its Mexican community, however, was mostly displaced to the adjacent Lower West Side community area, immediately to the south and southwest, better known as Pilsen, or later, as *La Dieciocho* (the Eighteenth Street Barrio). (De Genova 2005: 118)

To the north, Humboldt Park was the main home to the city's Puerto Rican population. Latino Chicagoans are segregated into three discrete pockets of the city: what was once the Puerto Rican-dominated Humboldt area in the city's near northwest side; the lower west side communities of Pilsen and *La Villita*; and the South Chicago eastside neighborhood that spreads over the border to the Indiana cities of East Chicago and Indiana Harbor. In all three areas, anywhere from 75 to 98 percent of the residents are Latino (US Census 2000):

> Between 1970 and 1980, in the historically most significant neighborhoods of Puerto Rican concentration on Chicago's Near Northwest Side (Humboldt Park, West Town, and Logan Square), the Mexican

population nearly quadrupled. . . . As of U.S. Census 2000, Mexicans had become the majority among Latinos in *all* of the historically Puerto Rican neighborhoods on the North Side, as well as in the adjacent areas of more recent Puerto Rican resettlement. (De Genova 2005: 119)

In 2008, Latinos comprised 27.8 percent of Chicago's population and with the significant African American population (35.3 percent) and other non-white groups, Anglos comprise only 31.5 percent of the city. The 778,000 Mexicans in Chicago are nearly equal to the number of Mexicans residing in Chicago's suburbs. The surrounding suburban communities of Cicero, Rosemont, Waukegan, Elgin, Addison, Aurora, and Chicago Heights are all between 25 and 50 percent Mexican. "Cicero, a city once comprised of a population predominately Italian and Eastern European, grew from 37% Latino in 1990 to 77%" in 2000 (Parra 2004: 15). Cicero's 66,000 Latinos are most often concentrated on the east side even though they comprise three-quarters of the population. The intense segregation within Chicago's city limits tends to be replicated in the Chicagoland suburbs as well. The dividing lines and resultant separation between Cicero's Latinos and non-Latinos cannot be more clearly mapped as the major dividing streets and other barriers keep the highest concentration of Anglos in the far southwest and the highest concentration of Latinos in the upper northeast. The recent work of Martínez (2009: 3) notes that the recent housing bust and foreclosure crisis are particularly pronounced in Chicago's Latino neighborhoods, where predominately Latino neighborhoods in Chicago and its suburbs "experienced reductions in values between 17 and 50 percent in the 2003–09."

Efforts by life-long Latina activist Emma Lozano in Chicago certainly exemplify the emerging political developments of coalition building and vivifying a sense of *Latinidad* as a grassroots movement. A former staffer in the Harold Washington Chicago mayoral administration, Lozano has worked tirelessly to develop three organizations working on behalf of immigrant rights. She is founder and president of the community-based membership organization *Pueblo Sin Fronteras* and two related non-profits, *Centro Sin Fronteras* and *Sin Fronteras*. One of the national leaders in the immigrant rights movement, she was recently recognized by the Cook County Board of Commissioners for her work on educational reform, legal advocacy for undocumented immigrants, and union representation regardless of citizenship status. She shares the stage with Middle Eastern and African American leaders to not only push the Chicago city council to urge the federal administration to repeal the Patriot Act, but also to identify and challenge the increased use of racial profiling as a result of the far-reaching powers of the Act.

More recently, Lozano and her spouse, Reverend Walter Coleman, arranged sanctuary for Elvira Arellano, who was scheduled to be deported due to her undocumented status though her seven-year-old son Saul was born in the United States and was thus a US citizen. Arellano is the president of *La Familia Latina Unida* that represents mixed-status Latino families. When Arellano left the church and toured the West Coast on behalf of immigrant rights, she was detained by Immigration and Customs Enforcement (ICE) agents in Los Angeles and deported on August 19, 2007.

At the national level, advocacy on behalf of Latinos is no better represented than long-time Chicago Congressional representative Luis Gutiérrez. As a representative of Chicago's Latino community, Gutiérrez, who hails from Puerto Rico, has built a career as one of the most prominent Latino representatives to Illinois' 4th district, which includes both the south-side Mexican and north-side Puerto Rican communities. As a result of responding to his varied constituencies, he is at the forefront and often the lone voice advocating for Latino issues, from progressive immigration reform, redress for Mexican *braceros*, to full citizenship rights for Puerto Ricans, and a myriad of pan-Latino issues.

Some of the most interesting manifestations of *Latinidad* or panethnic Latino identities are formed when different national origins communities find themselves experiencing the United States together. Ethnographic research by Ricourt and Danta (2003: xi) of Colombians, Ecuadorians, Chileans, Salvadorans,

Venezuelans, Argentinians, Bolivians, Uruguayans, Cubans, Dominicans, Puerto Ricans, and Mexicans in the Corona neighborhood of the Queens borough amply documents "*convivencia diaria,* or 'daily-life interaction', in apartments and houses, on the streets, in stores, in workplaces, and in churches . . . creating a unique Latino panethnic community." The shared public spaces of streets, schools, social service organizations, and parks are connected to the private spheres of residences, workplaces, churches, bodegas, and other ethnic shopping strips in shaping how these daily interactions develop a strong grassroots sense of *Latinidad* stemming from shared lived experiences.

The experiences and interactions indicative of Latinos living in Queens, New York are more likely to occur when new Latino immigrant groups are residing near one another in new destinations. For instance, the experience of being Salvadoran in Mexican Los Angeles or Nicaraguan in Cuban Miami are qualitatively different than being Latino in the Washington, DC metropolitan area or other new destinations in the South (such as Nashville, Tennessee; Atlanta or Dalton, Georgia; and Raleigh, North Carolina). As Latinos shift their destinations away from the major gateway cities, "immigration has shifted from being a regional phenomenon affecting a handful of states and a few metropolitan areas to a national phenomenon affecting communities of all sizes throughout all fifty states. . . . it was most evident among Mexicans and, to a lesser extent, other Latin Americans. . . . As a result of this unprecedented geographic transformation, millions of native white and black Americans found themselves directly exposed to the Spanish language and to Latin American culture for the very first time" (Massey 2008: 343).

Suro and Singer (2002) identify 18 cities experiencing "hypergrowth" as it relates to the growing Latino population from 1980 to 2000. "The Hispanic population grew by more than 300 percent – or twice the national average – after 1980. Altogether, the combined Hispanic population of all these metros jumped 505 percent between 1980 and 2000" (Suro and Singer 2002: 5). Table 2.7 notes that it is cities in Florida and North Carolina as well as re-emerging destinations such as Las Vegas, Providence, and

Minneapolis-St. Paul that comprise the new twenty-first-century gateways. The 2008 ACS data indicate that Mexicans comprise the majority of Latinos residing in new immigrant destinations, with the exception of the large Salvadoran presence in the Washington DC metro area (see table 2.8). Nearly every national origin group is represented in each of the new destinations and the possibilities are ripe for constituting destination-specific *Latinidades*. This is of course constrained by the lessons of Hazleton where neoliberal nativism reigns in ways that may tie Latinos together, but in a manner that is defined more by self-defense and reaction to imposed marginalization than by similar experiences, stemming from a coming together of their own volition, to create a shared sense of identity.

Conclusion

To fully recognize that *Latinidad* has a very long history of imposition does not negate the lived experiences of communities experiencing the United States similarly both by their own collective volition and also under the threat of nativist backlash. By understanding the role of intra-ethic organization that often bridges national origins communities by locating coalitions in political practice and daily experience, it makes sense that in the case of Hazleton, it was LatinoJustice, formerly the PRLDEF, that defended the full citizenship rights of all Latinos, regardless of their immigration or national origins status. " 'Latino' is short for *'latinamericano'*. Like its English counterpart, the term refers to the people who come from the territory in the Americas colonized by Latin nations, such as Portugal, Spain, and France, whose languages are derived from Latin. People from Brazil, Mexico, and even Haiti are thus all 'latinoamericanos'. Individuals who are descendents of the former British and Dutch colonies are excluded" (Oquendo 1998: 62). However, with the US Census equating Latino with Hispanic, the imposed categorization of Latino is very different from its derivations by groups that comprise the Latino category. *Latinidad*, in actual lived relations,

Table 2.7. "Hypergrowth"* New Latino Destinations, 2000

	Total Latino Population	Percent of Total Population	Percent Latino Growth, 1980–2000
Raleigh, NC	72,580	6	1180
Atlanta, GA	268,851	7	995
Greensboro, NC	62,210	5	962
Charlotte, NC	77,092	5	932
Orlando, FL	271,627	17	859
Las Vegas, NV	322,038	21	753
Nashville, TN	40,139	3	630
Fort Lauderdale, FL	271,652	17	578
Sarasota, FL	38,682	7	538
Portland, OR	142,444	7	437
Greenville, SC	26,167	3	397
West Palm Beach, FL	140,675	12	397
Washington, DC	432,003	9	346
Indianapolis, IN	42,994	3	338
Minneapolis-St. Paul, MN	99,121	3	331
Fort Worth, TX	309,851	18	328
Providence, RI	93,868	8	325
Tulsa, OK	38,570	5	303
Total	2,750,564	9	505

*Hypergrowth metros had Latino population growth over 300 percent between 1980 and 2000.
Source: Suro and Singer 2002: 6.

means that the broader Latin linguistic connection may hold sway, whereas at other times it might be only Spanish that bridges disparate communities into a common linguistic group. Chapter 3 points to the myriad of difficulties in building *Latinidades* from the ground up given the extremely varied pathways to citizenship that Latino immigrants must traverse in the process of becoming full rights-bearing US citizens.

Table 2.8. Latinos in Select New Destinations, 2008

	Atlanta–Sandy Springs–Marietta, GA Metro Area	Dalton, GA Metro Area	Athens–Clarke County, GA Metro Area	Durham, NC Metro Area
Total	5,251,899	133,072	186,095	478,299
Not Hispanic or Latino	*4,763,915*	*100,716*	*174,147*	*432,179*
Hispanic or Latino:	487,984	32,356	11,948	46,120
Mexican	299,120	28,227	6,994	30,585
Puerto Rican	32,793	445	296	2,225
Cuban	16,024	103	192	709
Dominican (Dominican Republic)	9,438	376	14	538
Central American:	67,919	2,360	2,347	8,185
Costa Rican	1,870			29
Guatemalan	20,703			2,079
Honduran	15,943			2,700
Nicaraguan	2,414			13
Panamanian	3,538			98
Salvadoran	22,605			3,107
Other Central American	846			159
South American:	40,919	114	1,584	2,296
Argentinian	2,316			257
Bolivian	195			148
Chilean	1,779			159
Colombian	16,981			974
Ecuadorian	3,094			289
Paraguayan	273			0
Peruvian	6,597			289
Uruguayan	2,715			0
Venezuelan	5,953			171
Other South American	1,016			9
Other Hispanic or Latino:	21,771	731	521	1,582
Spaniard	3,568			266
Spanish	3,005			196
Spanish American	309			0
All Other Hispanic or Latino	14,889			1,120

Source: US Census Bureau, 2006–8 American Community Survey.

Memphis, TN–MS–AR Metro Area	Washington–Arlington–Alexandria, DC–VA–MD–WV Metro Area	Nashville–Davidson–Murfreesboro–Franklin, TN Metro Area	Raleigh–Cary, NC Metro Area	Winston–Salem, NC Metro Area
1,278,634	5,306,742	1,518,971	1,043,281	461,154
1,230,152	4,673,343	1,438,953	952,991	419,736
48,482	633,399	80,018	90,290	41,418
36,810	103,255	51,213	58,708	30,059
1,910	41,070	4,118	6,521	2,091
1,145	13,545	1,598	1,991	468
138	13,415	321	1,862	552
5,136	286,831	15,112	10,372	5,014
42	2,859	321	482	70
757	42,723	5,530	1,753	1,436
2,171	28,246	3,210	3,022	367
165	10,818	552	167	271
557	5,048	247	334	126
1,336	190,478	5,192	4,233	2,619
108	6,659	60	381	125
1,347	118,267	3,499	5,508	2,298
33	8,209	99	565	157
93	33,260	210	248	0
55	6,038	88	184	0
437	19,053	960	1,917	442
29	8,091	764	449	413
0	1,383	11	14	9
181	33,191	616	1,109	878
190	2,122	30	130	84
167	3,176	512	719	299
162	3,744	209	173	16
1,996	57,016	4,157	5,328	936
489	6,986	294	499	108
288	9,010	711	722	233
0	565	5	53	28
1,219	40,455	3,147	4,054	567

3

Pathways to Citizenship

In the previous chapter, we discussed how Hazleton's hostile climate toward immigrants was the catalyst for bringing together Dominicans, Mexicans, Puerto Ricans, and other Latinos. In the process of mounting a political campaign to protect the rights of Latino immigrants, they overcame the tendency to have a Latino identity imposed upon them and in the process created a grass-roots sense of *Latinidad*. It is most relevant to note that a Puerto Rican advocacy organization is leading the way in protecting the rights of Latino immigrants (mostly Dominican, Mexican, and Colombian) and only federal pre-emption rules are currently providing a semblance of protection from hostility and fear aimed most often at "illegal Mexicans" but experienced by nearly all Latinos, regardless of citizenship and national origin status. Yet, varied claims on citizenship are paramount in terms of how Latino immigrants experience their reception upon arrival, and often shape their lived experiences well beyond initial entry.

Restrictionist immigration laws often rest on the assumption that entering the nation without proper documentation constitutes an abrogation of rights, even civil rights protection, afforded thereafter. Justice Munley pointed out this prevailing view in his dismissal of the Hazleton anti-immigrant ordinances:

> This argument appears to be a species of argument often heard in recent discussions of the national immigration issue: because illegal aliens broke the law to enter this country, they should not have any

legal recourse when rights due them under the federal constitution or federal law are violated. We cannot say clearly enough that persons who enter this country without legal authorization are not stripped immediately of all their rights because of this single illegal act. The Fourteenth Amendment to the United States Constitution provides that no State may "deprive any *person* of life, liberty or property, without due process of law; nor deny any *person* within its jurisdiction the equal protection of the laws." U.S. CONST. amend. XIV § 1. (Munley 2006: 43–4; emphasis added)

As a result, the prospect of reforming immigration law currently stands at a stalemate on the federal level. Both Democrats and Republicans are reluctant to enact the comprehensive immigration reform that has been introduced as bills in 2005 (McCain–Kennedy Bill), 2006, and 2007. Since then, more traction has been gained in the passage of laws restricting who can enter the country, fortifying the US–Mexico border, deporting undocumented immigrants, and punishing those who facilitate undocumented migration (employers, landlords, and smugglers or *coyotes*).

There is certainly an "idealized" image of immigrants assimilating into full-fledged citizens and that image is embedded in the European immigrant experience that individuals willingly and legally enter the nation (usually through Ellis Island), pay their dues, work hard, take their citizenship test, and then become American citizens. This image of old does not square with the contemporary reality of a broken immigration system that moves citizenship pathways to increasingly non-citizen or even illegal statuses. Not mentioned is the long-established second-class citizenship that Puerto Ricans experience as colonial citizens. Also ignored is the recent designation of Temporary Protected Status (TPS), in response to civil war, violence, and environmental disaster. In Central America, El Salvador was first designated as a result of civil war, and later Hurricane Mitch resulted in Honduras and Nicaragua being added to the list. Although Guatemala has experienced similar civil wars and national disasters, TPS has never been extended. Similarly, US-sponsored drug wars in Colombia and Peru have resulted in calls for TPS inclusion but to no avail.

For Latino immigrants, citizenship is key to a sense of national belonging. Given the impasse concerning US immigration reform, pathways to becoming US citizens are increasingly narrowed and negligible. What is experienced as a daily marker of exclusion or inclusion coincides with a resurgent scholarly interest in citizenship theory that has breathed new life into a concept central to several sociological traditions. Max Weber discussed citizenship and national belonging as a central marker of status. Without expressly deploying the terminology, W.E.B. DuBois nonetheless strongly criticized the second-class citizenship of African Americans in relation to the failed promises of Reconstruction and the institutionalization of Jim Crow segregation. Contemporary sociologists often reflect back to the origins of the British welfare state and the intellectual debates of the era that pitted revolutionary versus reformist Marxists. T.H. Marshall's three forms or theories of citizenship more broadly were embedded in the reformist approach of securing rights or goods for the working class to envision a more just and equal society. Marshall identified three forms of rights – civil, political, and social – and their associations are still sources of scholarly contention. Marshall seems to posit that the forms progress from civil liberties for the protection of the individual, to representative democracy and the right to vote, and finally to the most encompassing "whole range from the right to a modicum of economic welfare and security to the right to share to the full in the social heritage and to live the life of a civilized being according to the standards prevailing in the society" (Marshall 1964 [1950]: 92–3).

Ensuing debates juxtapose the idealized image of the individual rights-bearing citizen to abstract notions of "the common good" with obligatory, yet fleeting, cautions about the tyranny of the majority. "Citizenship, in sum, communitarians contend, should be an activity or a *practice* and not, as liberals hold, simply a *status* of membership. Precedence is to be given not to individual rights but to the pursuit of the common good" (Shafir 1998: 11; emphasis in original). Yet both liberal and communitarian political theories limit citizenship to national belonging and can be heavily criticized for their inability to theorize protections for those outside, or not members of, the political community. The role of immigrants, outsiders, temporary workers, and the stateless invokes criticisms of citizenship's supposed universality as clearly nation-state bounded and ultimately exclusionary of some residents' participation.

With this recognition in place, citizenship is then juxtaposed as a matter of status, rights, or identity (Joppke 2010). The analytical approaches to these three matters are exemplified by notions of national, postnational, and multicultural citizenship. Brubaker's national citizenship is, we contend, a reworking of Weber's notion of status that fully flushes out the question of belonging to the nation-state. Soysal's (1994) postnational citizenship is very much embedded in Habermas' (1998) recent engagement with the faltering place of nation-states in his longstanding defense of Enlightenment-inspired universal human rights. Kymlicka's (1996) multicultural citizenship is not as some often claim invoking the particularistic and historicized identities defended by Foucault in his famous debates with Habermas, as Kymlicka is clearly more interested in cautiously furthering the defense of individual rights and justice initiated by Rawlsian liberals (see Joppke 2010: 28). There is a fourth matter, particularly for Latino immigrant communities, defined by emerging approaches to cultural citizenship, which we will address in the next chapter.

Proponents of citizenship theory often identify four pathways to citizenship subscribed to depending upon a nation's history:

> *Jus soli*, or 'birthright citizenship', means that a person born on the given state's territory has the right to citizenship without further inquiry *Jus sanguinis* disregards territorial claims and bases the inheritance of citizenship on the citizenship status of one or both parents. A third form mixes these two ideas by requiring that a person be born in a given state and that either or both of the parents are also citizens or long-term legal residents of that state. The fourth method, naturalization, is the acquisition of citizenship by migrant foreigners. (Benhabib and Resnik 2009: 3)

The United States is often defined as a *jus soli* nation due to its inheritance from the French Revolution of the anti-aristocratic ideals that reduced citizenship status to bloodlines and replaced citizenship by birth on US soil as a guarantee in the US Constitution.

For present purposes, we define citizenship as the formal recognition of inclusion, rights, and status by the state that is embodied by practices of both inclusion and exclusion and resultant social locations along a continuum of citizenship statuses.

In the sociology of Latino immigration, this question of inclusion is embedded in two research questions: what conditions impel different national origin groups from Latin America to migrate to the United States and what are their conditions of reception? An oft repeated mis-specification stemming from these questions is the comparison of Cubans as political migrants to Mexicans as economic migrants (see Pedraza 1981, 1985; Portes and Bach 1985). Certainly for Cubans fleeing during the Revolution, they constitute political refugees or asylees. Many Mexicans migrate today in order to improve their economic situation and are not fleeing political persecution. Yet, it takes little work to uncover the historical and national variations that made Mexicans political "refugees" (well before the term was coined) during the Mexican Revolution (see Gamio 1931) and the Cuban exodus in the first part of the twentieth century that marked cigar makers and other Cuban workers in Key West, Tampa, and New York City as economic migrants.

Rather than making simple generalizations based on binary logic, there is a clear pole in the continuum of, on the one end, political refugees that find themselves welcomed with open arms to US society (e.g., first wave Cubans and Nicaraguans to south Florida during their respective revolutions) and, on the other end, the forms of "illegality" (De Genova 2005) for undocumented immigrants that fully marginalize and demonize most often working-class immigrants struggling to secure an economic foothold *without* the political protections of citizenship (e.g., twenty-first-century Mexican and Dominican working-class migrants). In the middle is a group who have been extended TPS as a result of this unwillingness to extend full inclusion based on the refugee model and thus unwilling to bend to the international human rights regime but at the same time unwilling to be ridiculed for the duplicity of extending rights to some, not to all, and not fully committing them to full marginalization that undocumented immigrants experience. Too often, citizenship status is contingent upon US foreign policy aims.

Temporary worker programs also do not fit with the idealized image of naturalization. Yet the reality is that since 1942 the US government has continuously provided a mechanism for, most often agriculture but other industries, access to employ temporary immigrant laborers. Two major programs (Bracero Program, 1942–64, and the H class work visas – H-2A, H2-B, and H-1B) have served as the major conduit for US employers to employ predominately, but not exclusively, Mexican immigrant labor. The last group that has seen its rights systematically diminished are those deemed "resident aliens" in the language of the Department of Homeland Security. For this group, commonly referred to as green carders (along with commuter migrants along the US–Mexico border), the process whereby one secures a green card and the cumbersome bureaucratic procedure of transferring one's status to naturalized US citizen point to the deepest flaws in the immigration system. The Diversity Visa Program (green card lottery) is for people from nations with low rates of residence in the United States. To give a sense of the demand and the small chance of entering the nation legally, less than 1 percent (a conservative estimate is just 0.87 percent or 0.5 percent if dependants of applicants are counted) of those who apply gain entry through the lottery. Every step of the process involved in securing permanent resident status and eventual US citizenship is compounded by multi-year waits (upwards of 8–14 years), cumbersome bureaucratic paperwork, fees, and delays that minimize the chances of becoming a legal US citizen. Resident aliens are also finding themselves imprecated in the politics of immigration and the rights accorded with permanent resident alien status are being stripped away with first California voters' attempt at passing Proposition 187 that informed the US Welfare Reform Act and then the Illegal Immigration Reform and Immigrant Responsibility Act (IIRIRA) that barred "legal immigrants" from receiving social benefits. Finally, the increasing illegality of those deemed "illegals," "illegal aliens," or other derogatory terms is evidenced by an increased militarization of the US–Mexico border, the rise in the immigration detention aspects of the prison-industrial complex, and legislative calls to make undocumented border-crossing a felony.

Table 3.1 identifies the continuum of Latino citizenship statuses that the US federal government extends to those deemed worthy or unworthy of naturalization. Current US naturalization law favors those with requisite employee skills in short supply or those with family members who are US citizens. Though there are restrictions for foreign nationals educated in the United States, as they are often not able to transfer student visas into work visas or apply for naturalization, the reality is the majority of those living legally in the United States are wealthy or middle-class professionals. Due to an incredible backlog of those who desire to become US citizens, the processing of citizenship claims is marred by bureaucratic inefficiency and claims are often denied due to trivial technicalities. As policy makers debate the politics of immigration, family reunification has become a perennial waiting game, though the 1965 Immigration and Nationality Act (INA) was designed with the lofty goal of first and foremost reuniting families who found themselves split by national borders. When those immigrants were from Ireland or other European nations, the system worked, but as more applicants came from Latin America or Asia, the bureaucratic commitment seemed to lag, as is evidenced today by the excessive wait times.

Working along the citizenship continuum, political refugees or asylum seekers are offered most of the protections afforded to naturalized citizens. We will discuss the Cuban refugee experience later but in addition to the 1966 Cuban Adjustment Act, the 1980 Refugee Act and 1997 Nicaraguan Adjustment and Central American Relief Act (NACARA) are extending a whole host of rights and protections to asylum seekers but always conditioned by US foreign policy interests. These interests are also what keep the United States invested in maintaining its colonial holdings – particularly the island of Puerto Rico. Colonial citizenship for Puerto Ricans means their ability to exercise their full rights is restricted to residing on the mainland. The history of acts and cases aimed at defining Puerto Rican citizenship is marked by a clearly defined second-class status where the

Table 3.1. Latino Citizenship Continuum

Naturalized Citizen	Political Refugee	Colonial Citizen	Temporary Protected Status	Temporary Visa Holder	Resident Alien	Undocumented Immigrant
1965 INA Family Reunification and Employee Skills	1966 Cuban Adjustment Act; 1980 Refugee Act; Nicaraguan (NACARA) Act 1997	Treaty of Paris; Foraker Act; Insular Cases; Jones Act; Commonwealth Act	DHS-TFS Designation 1990; INA, 8 USC section 1254a, 8 CFR Part 244	Bracero Program, 1942–64; H-2 Visa Program, 1986; IRCA (H-2A, H-2B, H-1B)	1986 IRCA; 1965 INA	Illegality – 1954 Operation Wetback; 1986 IRCA; 1996 IIRIRA
South America, middle-upper-class Latinos	Cuba and Nicaragua	Puerto Rico	El Salvador, Honduras, Nicaragua	Mexico, Argentina, Belize, Brazil, Chile, Costa Rica, Peru, Uruguay, Dominican Republic, Ecuador, El Salvador, Guatemala, Honduras, Nicaragua	"Green card" Latino immigrants, but same criteria as naturalized citizen	Mexico, Dominican Republic, Central America

interests of the colonizer define the lived experiences of the colonized. We will discuss (in relation to El Salvador) the recent development of extending TPS as a means of conforming to international human rights without committing to potential refugees even when they are fleeing persecution, if the persecutors align with US interests. TPS was extended to those fleeing violence or disasters from El Salvador, Honduras, and Nicaragua. The official definition is:

> Temporary Protected Status (TPS) is a temporary immigration benefit that allows qualified individuals from designated countries (or parts of those countries) who are in the United States to stay here for a limited time period. A country may be designated for TPS by the Secretary of Homeland Security based on certain conditions in the country that temporarily prevent the country's nationals from being able to return safely, or in certain circumstances, the country's government from being able to handle their return adequately. A TPS country designation may be based on on-going armed conflict, environmental disaster, or other extraordinary and temporary conditions in the country. (US Department of Homeland Security 2010)

Currently, TPS is scheduled to expire in March 2012 for Salvadorans and January 2012 for Hondurans and Nicaraguans. Finally, we will discuss the informalization of citizenship with the rise of temporary worker programs, the restrictions aimed at green card holders or "resident aliens," and undocumented migration in the context of deportation and militarization – or the rise in illegality.

In this chapter, we briefly discuss the laws that extended asylum and eventually full citizenship to some Cubans and its current retrenchment in the wet feet/dry feet policy of immigration enforcement agencies. Then we discuss the Salvadoran experience with TPS, which is also heavily informed by foreign policy concerns and the Cold War style politicization of those fleeing based on a well-founded fear of persecution. Finally, we discuss the increasing criminalization of immigration and how Mexicans in particular are subjected to the forms of neoliberal nativism that articulates undocumented status with full legal disenfranchisement.

Cubans and Refugee/Asylee Status

The 1966 Cuban Adjustment Act was one of the first laws to confirm the 1948 Universal Declaration of Human Rights and the 1951 United Nations Convention on the Status of Refugees. Article 14, paragraph 1, of the Declaration reads, "Everyone has the right to seek and to enjoy in other countries asylum from persecution." Article 1A, paragraph 1, of the 1951 Convention provides a "general definition of the refugee as including any person who is outside their country of origin and unable or unwilling to return there or to avail themselves of its protection, on account of a well-founded fear of persecution for reasons of race, religion, nationality, membership of a particular group, or political opinion." Though the UN was often looking to the past when designing an international human rights regime that included refugees (specifically aimed at the lack of international response to the German World War II Holocaust), the hope and idea was to never repeat the inaction that led to the loss of millions of lives.

The United States interpreted the reigning discourse on human rights and provided safe harbor with the framework of the Cold War squarely at the forefront. Consequently, when communist-supported forces aligned with Fidel Castro overthrew the Batista dictatorship in 1959, those sympathetic to Batista or not in favor of Castro sought refuge in the United States. Miami is only 200 miles from Cuba. On November 2, 1966, the US Congress passed Public Law 89-732, which states:

> the status of any alien who is a native or citizen of Cuba and who has been inspected and admitted or paroled into the United States subsequent to January 1, 1959 and has been physically present in the United States for at least one year, may be adjusted by the Attorney General, in his discretion and under such regulations as he may prescribe, to that of an alien lawfully admitted for permanent residence if the alien makes an application for such adjustment, and the alien is eligible to receive an immigrant visa and is admissible to the United States for permanent residence. Upon approval of such an application for adjustment of status, the Attorney General shall create a record of the alien's admission for permanent residence as of a date thirty months prior to

the filing of such an application or the date of his last arrival into the United States, whichever date is later. The provisions of this Act shall be applicable to the spouse and child of any alien described in this subsection, regardless of their citizenship and place of birth, who are residing with such alien in the United States.

The cumbersome bureaucratic complexity of securing refugee status was absolved with one act of Congress that legalized the status of all Cuban entrants, their spouses, and children, in what would serve as the model for the US treatment of political refugees thereafter.

The model that resulted was those seeking asylum from communist regimes would find it easy to regularize their status but if one was fleeing a US-sponsored dictatorship (which was often the case in Latin America), chances were slim that asylum would be granted. This approach would be tested in the 1980s under the Reagan administration. Reagan's foreign policy was based on the "domino" theory, which posited that communist movements in particular nations of the Third World would have the effect of pushing other nations along the same path of communist revolutionary movements rejecting capitalism as the mode of development. The Reagan administration went to great pains, covert and overt, to fund and arm political regimes supportive of US corporate interests and capitalist ideologies by squashing radical insurgent movements in Central America. As people fled the civil wars and violence, only those who supported capitalism and US aims, but were living in socialist nations such as Nicaragua, were given refugee status (at a rate of around 80 percent). Those attempting to escape state-sponsored death squads and violence in El Salvador and Guatemala were deemed economic migrants due to their governments' favorable status with the Reagan administration (refugee status approval rate closer to 2–3 percent). The selective application of this refugee status determination was almost wholly based on nation of origin and whether the current administration of that nation was on good terms with the present US administration or not. In 1997, the Clinton administration partially attempted to rectify the imbalance by supporting the passage of the Nicaraguan Adjustment and Central American Relief Act (NACARA), which increased the chances for Central Americans, other than Nicaraguans, to secure refugee status, or more often in the case of Salvadorans to qualify under what is referred to as Temporary Protected Status.

Cold War Politics, El Salvador, and Temporary Protected Status

In 1986, the United States had successfully stopped a leftist insurgency in El Salvador. By seeking Congressional support for military aid to the Salvadoran government, the Reagan administration strategically contained a rebellious push (Diskin and Sharpe 1986: 1). Amid this jockeying for power between the existing Salvadoran regime, the leftist rebels, and the US government, hundreds of thousands of Salvadorans were fleeing their war-stricken country. As the pace of this migration grew, the American government decided that while it might concern itself with Salvadoran politics, it could not be inconvenienced by Salvadoran citizens. As an extension of foreign policy, the United States crafted restrictive immigration policies toward Salvadorans in order to protect right-of-center national interests.

The onset of the Salvadoran civil war also sparked the beginning of a long line of US aid to the Salvadoran government. By late 1978, the Carter administration had become deeply concerned about the emerging developments in El Salvador. It was the administration's belief that the Salvadoran government's continued repression and opposition to reform would inevitably beget revolution. Carter, therefore, encouraged the regime to end its totalitarian practices and commence talks on reform. At the same time, Carter believed that if the country's extreme left gained significant power, US interests could be compromised. While the government's repressive stance was cause for concern, it was deemed preferable to a seizure of power by the radical left. To that end, military aid commenced flowing to the Salvadoran regime in order to stop any serious insurgency. Reagan took Carter's stance and extended it to include outright military intervention. The

Reagan administration was committed to the ultimate defeat of leftist forces. Reagan's focus on armed force resulted in his failure to support reform negotiations; in his view, rebels must simply be vanquished (Little 1994: 1–9).

To most Salvadorans, the civil war brought even greater hardship. Many faced forced recruitment into rebel forces, cross-fire, and the destruction of their homes and jobs. The result was a massive dislocation of Salvadoran citizens. Desperate to protect their own lives and those of their families, they fled El Salvador for Mexico, Honduras, and Belize. Some escaped to Canada, various European nations, and even Australia. The exodus would also result in a massive influx of Salvadorans into the United States. Only those few who owned property or were educated had permission to be in the country, so most sought *coyotes* (immigrant smugglers) to trek them from El Salvador through Guatemala and Mexico and into the United States. Once in the country, most refugees were able to find work and rent apartments. While there was the constant fear of being detained, most Salvadorans intended to return to their homeland after a year or two. In that time, they believed, the political situation would surely be resolved. Their legal status, therefore, was not of great importance. The continuous flow of migrants, however, though this was unknown at the time, would mark the beginning of a protracted balancing act involving US policies, the ever-changing political climate in El Salvador, and the response by Salvadoran people and those who sympathized with their cause. Most significantly for the United States, its policies in response to Salvadoran immigration began to reflect its policies toward El Salvador and the ongoing civil war.

The failure of the Reagan administration to support reform negotiations in El Salvador resulted in widespread criticism. By 1982, international pressure had mounted to the point that Reagan was forced to deny allegations that his strategy was predominantly military in origin. To bolster this denial, the administration began publicly supporting reform, democratization, and human rights. Secretly, however, aid to the Salvadoran regime continued. During the height of the war, between 1980 and 1990, US aid surpassed $5 billion (García 2006: 86). In 1981, Congress placed conditions

– called "certification requirements" – on aid to the Salvadoran regime. Particular conditions included protection of human rights, political security, and progress in democratization. These certification requirements became nothing more than a creative writing exercise for the State Department. In order to continue its aid, the administration claimed that there was indeed clear and ongoing progress in El Salvador. The 1984 election to select the president of El Salvador was heralded by the Reagan administration as evidence that its military aid was indeed in the service of establishing democracy, despite the fact that left-wing candidates were excluded from the ballot (Ferris 1987: 23). The administration now had the requisite political leverage to continue its fight against leftist insurgents. As a result, US policy – intentionally or not – had helped to strengthen the right and marginalize any reform efforts.

The most profound result of US policy was the human devastation wrought by the Salvadoran regime, funded as it was by American money and military. Violence in the streets reached horrific proportions, as depicted by Robert Armstrong and Janet Shenk (1982: 14): "Nor should it be difficult to reject the terror and barbarism of the Salvadoran armed forces: children impaled on the machetes of the National Guard; corpses beheaded and left lying on the streets; the skull of a man split open, a leaflet he was distributing stuffed in the wound; a woman raped by an entire platoon and then murdered, acid poured over her face to reveal death's hideous skull." Though certification requirements mandated that human rights must be demonstrably improved through US aid, the State Department merely claimed progress – a claim difficult to prove, as thousands of Salvadorans were being murdered at the hands of their own government. In 1983, the Reagan administration found that 30,000 political murders had occurred within the preceding three years, though they insisted that this constituted progress. By the end of the decade, nearly 75,000 Salvadoran citizens had been killed in the civil conflict.

Given this violence, a mass exodus of Salvadorans was almost inevitable. Initially, citizens in rural areas moved to urban centers to escape the near-constant bombings and battles. Though they had hoped to relocate temporarily within El Salvador, such optimism would prove to be futile. Soon, Salvadorans discovered that there was no safe harbor in their own country. Outward migration was the only means of escape. As this reality became clear, Salvadoran migrants set their sights on the United States.

Why the United States? The answer lies within the particular political, economic, and social hopes of the migrants. The United States offered the possibility of social stability and economic opportunity but the impetus for the Salvadoran exodus was safety. Contrary to what the Reagan administration asserted in its efforts to exclude those immigrants – namely, that Salvadorans were migrating to the US primarily for economic gain – financial stability was secondary to physical safety. Refugees from El Salvador only decided to flee their homeland when it became clear that violence had infiltrated every aspect of that homeland. They fled El Salvador to ensure their safety; they entered the United States because there was realistic hope of maintaining financial solvency and enjoying basic social liberties (Mahler 1995: 56).

Fewer than 25 percent of Salvadorans arrived in the United States legally; that is, with valid visas or with refugee status. Some entered with a temporary visa and simply stayed once their visas expired, but the majority – close to 800,000 – entered illegally (Mahler 1995: 4). Many Americans were less than enthusiastic about the arrival of nearly 1 million Salvadorans, believing that they would present a drain on the economy. Reaffirming many prejudicial or inflammatory beliefs, the Reagan administration tried to discourage the early migrants. President Reagan argued that there was little need for the Salvadorans to travel all the way to the United States in search of something they could gain south of the border. After all, the US was actively promoting economic stability in all five countries in Central America – including El Salvador. Thus, it was widely believed (and the Reagan administration encouraged this belief) that Salvadoran migrants were seeking economic gain, not fleeing war and oppression. Salvadorans faced hostility based on the misperception that they were simply trying to exploit America's goodwill and affluence.

In 1987, Congressman Claude Pepper spoke to the "economic migrant" ruse during a Congressional hearing on Salvadoran deportation: "In the El Salvadoran instance, the Government has not indicated any disposition to allow the people from El Salvador who are in the United States to remain here until they feel they can safely return to their home." Congressman Pepper went on to discuss a bill that would ultimately allow Salvadoran refugees to stay: "What I want to emphasize is that we are not here to protect these people who are fleeing in order to get an economic advantage in our country. We are trying to protect these people who are being required to return home where they are in danger of their lives or their liberty, and we feel that they are entitled to sanctuary in our country" (Storrs 1987: 99).

Though deportation was a real threat, Salvadorans felt they could fly under the government radar because the Immigration and Naturalization Service (INS) did not single them out for enforcement. Thus, while the Reagan administration favored deportation, the INS did not pay them special attention. Many Salvadorans were able to find work, attend school, rent apartments, and obtain a driver's license or identification card. Some were even fortunate enough to gain legal advice and apply for political asylum. Such applications, however, were rarely successful: almost 99 percent were denied (Coutin 2007: 48). The restrictions placed on Salvadoran immigration worsened with the 1986 Immigration Reform and Control Act (IRCA). This Act imposed sanctions on any employer who knowingly hired an undocumented worker. Furthermore, IRCA called for the establishment of an employment authorization document. These restrictions were at least somewhat offset by IRCA's creation of an amnesty program for any illegal Salvadoran who had been continuously present in the United States since 1982. Under the amnesty program, nearly a quarter of a million Salvadorans were able to legalize their status (García 2006: 91). Such legalization represented permanent residency and eventual citizenship. The majority of Salvadoran immigrants, though, faced serious adverse effects from the newly passed immigration reform. The Act presented new obstacles in undocumented Salvadorans' efforts to find work, and those who lacked an authorization document or work permit had few employment options. Ultimately, IRCA was an effective way for the United States to inhibit illegal immigration by halting access to work (Coutin 2003: 516).

Salvadorans, then, experienced American life on the margins. Many spoke limited English; had few resources with which to establish any financial security; and now had to provide particular credentials in order to obtain a job. By the mid-1980s, however, a counter-movement of sorts had taken hold. This grassroots effort, called the "the Sanctuary Movement" (based upon biblical scripture of using the church to provide safe passage for those persecuted under unjust and oppressive laws), was created to assist Salvadoran immigrants, even if it meant disobeying the US government. Efforts included harboring and transporting Salvadoran immigrants as well as providing financial assistance. Initially, the Sanctuary Movement was supported by a few community groups. A few years later it enjoyed the support of over 200 individual churches and the endorsement of over 20 religious associations (García 2006: 108). The result was a sizable group of US citizens who challenged the foreign policy and selective application of immigration and refugee laws by providing sanctuary for those fleeing the violence of US-sponsored military regimes. The Sanctuary Movement also counted among its supporters Latino-serving organizations, some universities and university towns, and eventually the state of New Mexico when then-Governor Toney Anaya declared the state as sanctuary (MacEoin 1985).

Elie Wiesel, a member of the movement and former Holocaust refugee, proclaimed: "From the ethical perspective, it is impossible for human beings today, especially for my contemporaries, who have seen what people can do to themselves and do to one another, not to be involved." He went on to add: "If the American people were made aware – through newspapers and through television – of what is happening, if they were shown the suffering of the refugees, they would move Congress to act" (cited in Chmiel 2001: 66–7). The Sanctuary Movement was an ethical and moral response to the Reagan administration's denial of refugee status for Salvadorans. Its members acted out of their conviction that, contrary to the official government stance, Salvadorans were in fact fleeing war and oppression. Sanctuary Movement activists believed that the Reagan administration's denial of refugee status was a violation of the Geneva and Helsinki Accords, the UN Convention on Refugees, and the United States' own 1980 Refugee Act. These national and international legislations clearly defined the terms by which a migrant could obtain refugee status, terms that the Reagan administration attempted to ignore. The Sanctuary Movement, then, also attempted to draw attention to the administration's unfair application of the "economic migrant" argument in denying asylum to Salvadoran refugees. The Sanctuary Movement created the impetus for the government and the courts to reconcile the interpretation of immigration, deportation, and refugee laws.

The efforts of the Sanctuary Movement resulted in Salvadorans gaining certain protections in US society. A particularly illuminating event came in the form of a lawsuit known as the "ABC case." The lead plaintiff, the American Baptist Church, sued the US government for discriminating against Salvadoran asylum applicants. The basis of the suit was the allegation that the Reagan administration had willfully ignored the 1980 Refugee Act. Lawyers for the plaintiff argued that Salvadorans were being treated unfairly and were victims of political bias in the asylum process. The result was an out-of-court settlement that granted many Salvadorans the right to asylum interviews that would ensure fair consideration of their claims (Coutin 2003: 512). The settlement acknowledged the negligence of the administration in considering all relevant factors involved in asylum and deportation decisions. Moreover, the settlement noted, the Reagan administration had ultimately failed to recognize Salvadorans' legitimate claims for political asylum.

The 1990s would prove to be a watershed decade for Salvadorans. In 1990, Congress passed a new Immigration Act. The Act effectively increased the number of legal immigrants allowed into the United States each year. It also created Temporary Protected Status (TPS) and designated Salvadorans as the first recipients of that status. In order to be eligible, Salvadorans must have been present in the United States since September 29, 1990. The temporary status was scheduled to expire in June

1992. Finally, the government agreed to put a halt to its policy of detaining and deporting most Salvadoran immigrants.

The applications of the ABC case results and the 1990 Immigration Act posed a dilemma for the US government. The United States had consistently supported the authoritarian, right-wing Salvadoran government. At the same time, the US asylum process asked applicants to prove a well-founded fear of persecution if they were forced to return home. Of course, asylum seekers were expected to apply for refugee status before entering the United States – an untenable situation for those fleeing wars and violence. The new policy – more amenable to asylum applications – amounted to an admission that the United States supported a government that violated its own citizens' human rights. In response to asylum settlements, lawyer Marc Van Der Hout observed: "These settlements are a major victory for all Salvadorans in this country whose claims for political asylum were being summarily denied for purely political reasons." Van Der Hout continued: "The tragedy, however, is that it took ten years for the government to reverse its policy of putting support for the military Government of El Salvador over its human rights obligations to grant asylum to legitimate refugees" (cited in Bishop 1990).

The end of the Cold War seriously threatened US rationale for continuing its military support of the El Salvadoran regime. The East–West battle that the Reagan administration used to justify its actions was no longer valid, and any further action would be nothing more than an expensive nuisance. In February 1991 Luigi Einaudi, US Ambassador to the Organization of American States, addressed the situation thus: "A negotiated political solution and a cease-fire leading to free elections should be at the top of our regional agenda. All sides need to put maximum efforts to achieve peace within a democratic framework and justice now. The United States commits itself to support these efforts." On April 7, 1992, President George Bush officially notified Congress of a peace agreement in El Salvador (Little 1994: 73–4).

With peace declared in their homeland, Salvadorans could ostensibly return home without fear of violence or reprisal. Many, however, had already established themselves in the United States and expressed little desire to return to a country whose government had visited such horror upon its own people. Moreover, the peace agreement meant a new set of legal obstacles to negotiate. Applications such as TPS and the ABC settlement were designed to address the specific needs of a specific type of migrant: a refugee who was fleeing war and political persecution at home. Community organizations focused on Salvadoran protection negotiated new ways that undocumented immigrants could become US citizens. These groups lobbied heavily for an extension of the Temporary Protected Status program. As TPS was set to expire, the INS and State Department decided to allow Salvadoran TPS recipients to register for Deferred Enforced Departure (DED). DED, in turn, was scheduled to expire on January 31, 1996 – the same deadline for ABC class-action suit members to file for political asylum (Coutin 2007: 58–60). A further burden to Salvadoran immigrants hoping to stay in the United States came with the passage of the Illegal Immigration Reform and Immigrant Responsibility Act (IIRIRA) in 1996, which made it more difficult to obtain legal residency. The following year, however, the NACARA, as well as a series of administrative concessions, guaranteed eventual permanent residency for ABC class-action suit members (Coutin 2003: 508–13).

Considering the urgent, typically dangerous circumstances of migration, most Salvadorans left their homeland with little planning and limited availability to those resources necessary to establish any financial or social network. Fortunately for these migrants, many activists in the United States were committed to their assistance. Los Angeles, in particular, acted as a hub for activist efforts, as the above data from 1990 show. Agencies such as *El Rescate* and the Central American Resource Center (CARECEN) were established in Los Angeles as grassroots organizations to assist Salvadorans and other Central Americans who fled their war-stricken countries. These organizations played critical roles in creating self-help and social service programs for Salvadoran migrants. Other goals of such organizations included establishing political networks, challenging immigration policies, and spreading the message of the Salvadorans' human rights story. The transmission of that story, told as it was through available media outlets, served the singular purpose of raising broader awareness of Salvadorans' experience (Hamilton and Chinchilla 2001: 119–52).

Susan Bibler Coutin examines the Salvadoran experience in terms of their "spaces of nonexistence." She explains that Salvadorans can be physically present and socially active in the United States but often lack the full legal status to reside in the country. Conversely, Salvadorans can live in El Salvador with full legal permission; due to repression and persecution, however, humanity and meaningful citizenship are negated. There are multiple forms in which nonexistence takes place, ranging from social isolation to physical destruction to legal and political removal. As noted previously, many Salvadorans fled to the United States to escape persecution and violence in El Salvador. Once in the US, Salvadorans found themselves marginalized. Yet, Salvadorans are not fully confined to these spaces of nonexistence. They take part in a myriad of day-to-day activities: they have jobs; they rent apartments and buy property; they go to school; they get married. Legal nonexistence, however, can lead to detainment and deportation back to the life-threatening conditions in El Salvador. This legal nonexistence "can mean working for low wages in a sweatshop or being unemployed. It can mean the denial of medical care, food, social services, education, and public housing. And it can mean an erasure of rights and personhood" (Coutin 2003: 517–21).

Mexican Illegality and Informal Citizenship

The major trend in US immigration law, since its monumental liberalization in the 1965 Hart–Cellar Immigration and Nationality Act, has been to scale back the opportunities for securing citizenship and either informalizing or criminalizing the flow of in-migrants. Informalization relates to the development of guest-worker or temporary visa programs that do not confer access to permanent citizenship status, nor are the programs designed to extend even a semblance of the full rights accorded US citizens. This began with the US–Mexico Bracero Program, which was the first temporary worker program in the world, which began in 1942 and continued until 1964. (The program was named after the term *bracero* referring to arms or *brazos* in Spanish and translating as worker.) Designed to be a wartime labor relief measure, agricultural producers successfully pressured the United States into extending the program for 22 years. During that time, 4.5 million individual work contracts were signed by approximately 2 million Mexican farmworkers. During World War II, the US railroad industry also employed *braceros*. The vast majority of workers went to three states (California, Arizona, and Texas) but 30 US states participated in the program, while every state in Mexico sent workers northward. Workers were severely disempowered in their attempts to secure the rights guaranteed to them in the agreements made between the two governments.

The Bracero Program began on August 4, 1942, in Stockton, California, as a result of the US government responding to requests by Southwest growers to recruit foreign labor. Nine months later the railroad industry secured the importation of Mexican laborers to meet wartime shortages. The Bracero Program involved only men, not their families. It was also highly regimented because *braceros* were supervised by the US government and grower associations throughout their movement in America (Perea 1997: 235–6).

When the Bracero Program originally passed, the US government and many growers were accepting of the program and the influx of Mexican contract laborers entering the United States. Many US growers were afraid that the war would limit the number of laborers that could work on their farms. If this occurred, there would not be enough workers to harvest the crops on these farms and the crops would rot. The Bracero Program was established in order to combat the lack of farmworkers. However, there were mixed feelings among the growers when the Bracero Program was established and many growers were outwardly hostile to the arrangements. The growers had hoped that the Bracero Program would mirror a similar program that occurred after World War I in which America reduced the amount of limitations put on contract laborers and granted the growers a large hand in the operations. However, Mexico no longer played such a submissive role in the affairs of Mexican contract laborers.

Mexican government officials, under the auspices of the guideline that explicitly banned discrimination against Mexican nationals, used it as the key bargaining chip to promote the decent treatment of *braceros* by US growers. From 1942 to 1947, no *braceros* were sent to Texas because of documentation of such mistreatment. Only after a series of anti-discrimination assurances by the Texas government were growers allowed to import *braceros*. The Mexican government also blacklisted Colorado, Illinois, Indiana, Michigan, Montana, Minnesota, Wisconsin, and Wyoming until the 1950s, due to discriminatory practices documented in those states.

After potential *braceros* secured the necessary paperwork from local officials, their first stop was in Mexico at recruitment centers designed to assemble a qualified labor force of experienced male workers, who were assigned numbers and processed by that number. Next, in the US processing centers, the men stripped for inspection for hernias, sexually transmitted diseases, and communicable diseases such as tuberculosis. If they passed, a delousing spraying with DDT followed before they dressed. The weeding out of "undesirables" even included inspections of workers' calloused hands to ensure they were adept at agricultural tasks. Representatives of growers' associations then chose which men they would employ as workers and the work they would do.

The transportation, housing, and boarding of *braceros* were extensions of batch-handling. Living conditions for *braceros* were similar to the military, as they typically lived in barracks complete with a mess hall that served institutionally prepared meals. Less desirable living arrangements included tents, chicken coops, barns, Japanese internment camps, high school gymnasiums, and stockyards. If *braceros* lodged a complaint about negative treatment, they had to fear reprisal in the form of deportation. No shifts to other jobs were possible because contracts explicitly tied them to a specific employer, and *braceros* were powerless to negotiate with their employers.

Given limited options for active protest, *braceros'* main form of resistance was the exit option. Low wages, bad food, excessive deductions from paychecks, poor housing, domineering supervisors, or on-the-job injuries prompted many *braceros* to leave their contracts. An estimated 20–33 percent "skipped" on their contracts, or in other words exited the Bracero Program. A significant (but uncounted) number who remained for the duration of the contract thereafter refused to return to the United States in subsequent seasons.

In the summer of 1954, Operation Wetback was implemented and around 800 Border Patrol officers traveled throughout the southern border of the United States. These officers used raids and road blocks to obtain and deport undocumented workers in the United States (Hernández 2006). The Border Patrol officers utilized around 300 buses, jeeps, cars, and also some seven planes to search for "wetbacks" on US soil (Ngai 2004: 155–6). At this time, the term wetback was used to refer to the illegal Mexican workers in the United States.

In an attempt to end the illegal trafficking of immigrant workers who were not granted work under the Bracero Program, President Eisenhower used approximately 1,075 Border Patrol agents in total to detect and deport the hundreds of thousands of Mexican immigrants (mostly undocumented but the dragnet also caught citizens, *braceros*, and legal immigrants as well). By the end of that July, more than 50,000 Mexicans were apprehended in Arizona and California by the Border Patrol and approximately 488,000 Mexican immigrant workers had left the country due to the threat of being arrested. At this time, the Border Patrol agents were also moving into Texas, Idaho, Nevada, and Utah. In September, it was estimated that nearly 80,000 were detected in Texas alone and between 500,000 and 700,000 Mexican laborers freely left this state. Once these illegal workers were taken into custody, they were transported by bus or by train deep into Mexico so they could not easily re-enter the United States by crossing the border. In addition, tens of thousands of these individuals were taken by boat back to Mexico (Dillin 2006). The US Border Patrol worked alongside the Mexican government in order to apprehend and deport illegals in the United States. The contradiction of mass deportations occurring during a period of state recruitment of temporary laborers represents a pattern of marginalization long unique to Mexican immigrants but increasingly applied in immigration law since the Bracero Program/Operation Wetback era.

When the Bracero Program was terminated in 1964, immigration law was overhauled for the first time since the Quota Acts with the passage of the INA of 1965. Since it removed discriminatory quotas, the Act is often hailed as part of the civil rights legislation. One provision extended the Bracero Program with the development of an H-2 temporary visa program. The H-2 (after 1986, the H2-A) program served largely as the safety valve for large-scale agribusiness and its desire for cheap, pliable, temporary labor. The H-2 program was severely underutilized because the other, less bureaucratic option, hiring undocumented immigrants, was never deemed illegal or worthy of sanction until the 1986 Immigration Reform and Control Act. The H-2A program was reauthorized in IRCA and actually expanded to include H-1B (specialty occupations) and H-2B (wage-shortage industries) temporary migrants as well. The key to temporary visa programs is that the US government (and by extension employers) are not responsible for the long-term needs of a significant class of laborers and thus are not required to extend the full rights of citizenship (or economic security) in this more informal arrangement.

The H-2A program allowed growers access to a steady stream of temporary labor if they were willing to meet the bureaucratic requirements. They were required to provide free and adequate housing, and code inspectors were quite thorough. As a result, H-2A farm labor camps often offered better housing than that hitherto available to migrants. Growers also had to adhere to an adverse effect wage rate and ensure that working conditions did not deter domestic interest. Interviews with the Department of Labor and lawyers from US Sugar Corporation estimate that in 1992 there were 19,000 H-2A laborers, primarily Jamaicans and Haitians working on the East Coast. Mainly employed in Florida by US Sugar, as it was the last corporation to mechanize production, 4,300 sugar workers were joined in the H-2A program by 1,145 sheep herders in Montana and 2,800 apple pickers in New York. From 1982 to 1991, Florida's sugarcane producers employed 10,000 H-2A workers per year but mechanization has led to steady decline and a now nonexistent labor demand.

Over the past ten years, the H-2A program has primarily been utilized by the tobacco industry. Public data made available in 2003 show that agricultural firms in all 50 states employ H-2A labor. In 2002, there were 42,000 visas issued, which increased to 45,000 in 2003. Tobacco is the largest single crop that employs H-2A workers, with tobacco workers constituting 35 percent of all H-2A visas. Tobacco growers are primarily in North Carolina, Kentucky, and Virginia. Though the US Department of Labor (DOL) does not make the data readily and publicly available, it is widely acknowledged by scholars and labor activists that Mexican workers are the main visa recipients. The Global Workers Justice Alliance estimates 88 percent of H-2A workers are Mexican according to their analysis of 2006 DOL data (40,283 of 46,432 visa holders). They estimate that Mexicans are certified for 82 percent of all H-2 visas in 2009. Nearly one-fourth of all workers are contracted to farms in North Carolina.

Yet, the vast majority of temporary workers come through the H-1B program, which is currently capped at 195,000 entries. Social scientist Rafael Alarcón refers to these specialized workers, primarily computer engineers and scientists, as *cerebreros* due to their recruitment for mental labor. A small, but significant, contingent of Mexican citizens have entered the United States on H-1B temporary visas but the majority of recipients are from India, China, and Great Britain. In FY2000, approximately 144,000 specialized workers were recruited in the H-1B program. The number of those positions certified by the DOL jumped to 728,269 in 2007 (US Department of Labor 2009).

The H-2B program is the leftover category for temporary entry as long as an employer demonstrates no native workers are willing to take the jobs at the prevailing wage. Landscaping, hotel cleaning, and other seasonal occupations, which traditionally relied upon undocumented Mexican labor, comprise the majority of the 66,000 eligible visa recipients. As of January 2010, the US Department of Labor identified the following nations eligible to apply for H-2A and B visas. Of the 39 eligible nations, those in Latin America include Argentina, Belize, Brazil, Chile, Costa Rica, Dominican Republic, Ecuador, El Salvador, Guatemala, Honduras, Mexico, Nicaragua, Peru, and Uruguay. The types of labor performed under the H-2B visa system include construction tasks (asphalt and paving contractors, masonry contractors, framing, and roofing); landscaping; timber and lumber; manufacturing, maintaining, and installing seasonal items; seasonal retail and wholesale (nurseries and garden centers, food processing and produce packing, seafood processing and fish packing, resorts, restaurants, and hotels, tent erection and other special event companies). In 2007, the DOL certified 254,615 positions under the H-2B program. The top six employers of H-2B workers include (1) the Brickman Group, which hired 3,020 landscapers and groundskeepers; (2) the Vail Corporation, hiring 1,988 sports instructors, housekeepers, and short order cooks; (3) Trugreen Landcare, which hired 1,731 landscapers and groundskeepers; (4) Marriott International, which hired 1,696 housekeepers, dining room attendants, and kitchen helpers; (5) Eller & Sons Trees, hiring 1,433 forest workers and tree planters; and (6) Agricultural Establishment Landscapes Unlimited, hiring 1,358 landscapers and groundskeepers (US Department of Labor 2009).

With approximately 10 million undocumented workers residing in the United States, clearly these temporary visa programs are not being utilized by the majority of employers who hire immigrants. Yet, temporary status in the United States is not the same as having access to citizenship or "resident alien" (green card) status. Temporary visa holders are still expected to return to their nation of origin once their short-term hire expires. Many corporations also rely upon the same laborers from year to year, or they offer more permanent employment options even though it often means workers risk deportation and disbarment for overstaying their visa. The reality is that for most Latin American immigrants, a broken immigration system means accepting temporary visas or entering the country without documentation as their only viable means of working and living in the United States.

Beyond informalization, a more nefarious approach that the US government is currently deploying is the criminalization of immigrants. Partially to assuage what we discuss in chapter 5 as the rise in neoliberal nativism, criminalization entails a major departure from how immigrants were conceptualized previous to the 1970s (when there was no such thing as an "illegal"). Shifting discourse about an act (and a civil offense at that – not a criminal act) and turning it into a noun as in a person or more often a thing, the language that deems undocumented border-crossers to be "illegals" is too often reinforced and reified by public commentators who spin the anti-immigrant rhetoric.

A quick sampling of evening Fox News commentary demonstrates both the frequent vilification of those characterized as "illegal" and the duplicitous lack of accountability or consistency in holding those responsible for creating the labor demand in the first place. In October 2010, news broke that anti-immigrant ideologue Lou Dobbs had been hiring undocumented workers to tend his estate and horse farms. Appearing on Bill O'Reilly's program, O'Reilly chastised Dobbs, stating: "With your profile of being against hiring illegal aliens, you should say you want all legal workers on your property and if it happens again they're fired."[7] Though the quote appears to hold the xenophobic Dobbs accountable for hiring undocumented workers (Dobbs claimed he hired a landscaping firm and thus had no idea the company's workers were undocumented), the naturalization of the term "illegal aliens" restores the reified representation of unwanted, criminal others not of this nation. The anti-immigrant sentiments are mutually reinforcing of the actions by the Minutemen vigilantes who seek to control the border and keep "illegals" out. The construction of illegality shifts the blame from faulty government policies or unscrupulous employers and onto the immigrants solely, who are then the only ones punished for all the complex relations embedded in "illegal" immigration. "Moreover, the spatialized condition of 'illegality' reproduces the physical borders of nation-states in the everyday life of innumerable places throughout the interiors of the migrant-receiving states. Thus, the legal production of 'illegality' as a distinctly spatialized and typically racialized social condition for undocumented migrants provides an apparatus for sustaining their vulnerability and tractability as workers" (De Genova 2002: 439).

Most often the images of illegality are unauthorized border-crossings, workplace raids, neighborhood sweeps, and mass deportations. As a result of the near-exclusive focus on the US southern border, "illegal" becomes synonymous with Mexican. Yet, other Latino immigrant groups are similarly situated in terms of their undocumented status and subjection to the cycle of unauthorized entry, detention, and deportation. Dominicans and Salvadorans have recently made news due to their shared experience with the Department of Homeland Security (DHS) ramping up the deportation of "criminal aliens," who are now one of the easiest to deport and dually stigmatized groups. Felony convictions can lead from five-year to lifetime bars on entry into the United States, and often being deported as a "criminal alien" results in a period of incarceration in one's country of origin.

Additionally, crime waves in the Dominican Republic and El Salvador are often blamed on the deportees, regardless of the validity of the claim, which has far-reaching consequences on their ability to reintegrate into society, get a job, etc. The *Christian Science Monitor* covered the case of Dominican Freddy Muñoz, who was deported as a permanent resident alien because of a drug conviction. "In many cases, those deported never considered themselves anything other than Americans. Muñoz, born in Santo Domingo, moved to New York with his parents when he was 8 years old. He went to PS 128, scalped tickets at Yankee stadium, and had a job working in the laundry room of a health club. After leaving as a child, he only visited the Dominican Republic once before being deported. . . . 'We are not liked here. And no matter how we try, we can't get jobs,' says Muñoz. 'I hustle here, hustle there . . . sometimes I do a paint job. Sometimes my aunt helps me out. Mainly, I have nothing.'"[8]

The *Los Angeles Times* published an in-depth analysis of the Salvadoran street gang *La Mara Salvatrucha*, or MS-13, and their increasing presence in the jails of El Salvador. The story discusses the merry-go-round effect of gang members deported as criminal aliens, finding themselves in the urban locales of El Salvador both ostracized and unfamiliar with a nation they rarely call home, and finding the binational network of MS-13 as their only source for social support. "The effects of deportations and continuing MS-13 recruitment rippled across El Salvador to places like San Miguel, an agricultural hub and the country's third-largest city. The area has become both a base of the gang's strength and a pivot point in the group's spread to the Washington area."[8] The deportations seem to have the unintended consequence of actually increasing gang membership due to the stigmas deportees face in both worlds. A gang that was born out of the ashes of El Salvador's civil war, initially populated by US government-trained death squad members, and adeptly changing their military uniforms for tattoos, shaved heads, and criminal syndicates, now counts as its base of operations Cuidad Barrios (a prison in San Miguel, El Salvador that houses convicted MS-13 gang members).

The vast majority of those deported are not criminals and the only offense they have committed is crossing a border in the attempt to secure an economic livelihood for their families. This goal has been increasingly thwarted by the deadly practice of militarizing the border. The terminology of "sweeps" and "operations" is deployed by Immigration and Customs Enforcement (formerly the INS) in a clearly military-style practice of population containment, followed by forcing those deemed undesirable over the border via bus, boat, train, and air lifts. Sociologist Timothy Dunn (1996) has quite successfully argued that the military doctrine of low-intensity conflict (LIC) has been applied by the US Immigration and Naturalization Service to "defend" the southern border of the United States. The equipment used to patrol the border (helicopters, night-vision equipment, electronic intrusion-detection ground sensors), operational tactics and strategies of border enforcement (combining police, military, and paramilitary forces), and the overall aim of social control of a targeted civilian population all embody the LIC doctrine that has been put into action by the US military in Vietnam, Afghanistan, Iraq, Somalia, Libya, Kuwait, Panama, and Grenada.

What has become the most visible physical manifestation of this militarization of the border region has been the construction of walls and fences to separate the urban sister cities. A series of INS/ICE campaigns from 1993 to the present (such as Operation Blockade and Operation Hold-the-Line in El Paso, Operation Gatekeeper in San Diego, and Operation Guardian – "Light up the Border" campaign in Douglas and Operation Safeguard in Nogales, Arizona) have all had the result of physically defining the line in the sand or rivers that have symbolically marked the divisions between Mexico and the United States. A study by the American Civil Liberties Union and Mexico's National Commission on Human Rights estimated over 5,600 deaths are attributed to raising the stakes and dangers associated with illicit border-crossing (Jimenez 2009). The shifting of entry points to the high mountain deserts of East San Diego County or the Arizona-Sonora desert has made border-crossing increasingly deadly.

With increased policing of the border, those detained are finding that with criminalization comes incarceration. "The prisoners are held in the INS's [ICE] service processing centers; in local jails; in facilities owned and operated by private prison companies such as the Corrections Corporation of America (CCA), the Wackenhut Corporation [now GEO Group], and the Correctional Services Corporation (CSC); and in Bureau of Prisons facilities, including federal penitentiaries. Wherever they are held, INS prisoners are 'administrative detainees'; they are not serving a sentence" (Dow 2004: 9). Only immigrants accused of unauthorized entry find themselves without the civil liberties afforded to citizens who are accused of committing crimes. Undocumented immigrants find they can be held without warrant or just cause and "indefinitely detained" as we learned after the 9/11 roundups of "suspected terrorists" who were not held as prisoners of war, or even as enemy combatants, but who were sometimes detained due to immigration status violations. This fallacious conflation of illegal immigration with terrorism follows a long line of fallacious links that connected immigration with the social evils of the day –

including drugs when the War on Drugs was declared and in past generations with health scares such as typhoid fever. The difference today is the money to be made in the detainment industry:

> The need for immigrant detention space dramatically increased after 9/11. The government began to target noncitizens with mass arrests during sweeps through immigrant communities, increased prosecutions of undocumented border crossers, and the deliberate use of immigration law to hold people while looking for criminal or terrorist charges against them. . . . The average time an immigrant is detained is 42.5 days from arrest to deportation. To detain an immigrant at $85 per day equals $3,612.50 per detainee. In 2003 DHS was holding 231,500 detainees, and the budget to cover this was $1.3 billion . . . [and] there was more than $50 million slated for the construction of immigrant jails. (Fernandes 2007: 193–4)

The rise in immigration detentions is quickly filling the void left by the decreasing crime rate and today's prisoners that fuel the prison-industrial complex are increasingly the undocumented economic migrants who find their pathways to citizenship are mostly a dead end.

The best example of this can be found today in Miami's Krome Detention Center, which is discussed in both Dow and Fernandes. The majority of detainees are Cubans and Haitians seeking refuge but who often find themselves "indefinitely detained." "Detainees who came here during the 1980 Mariel boatlift are probably the most lasting victims of US immigration detention" (Dow 2004: 16). The quintessential political migrants from a nation designated as a state sponsor of terrorism, Cuba, are finding themselves less and less able to translate a sympathetic foreign policy climate into easier access to citizenship. Since the Clinton administration, Cubans have been received by what is one of the wackiest criteria for admission, known as the wet feet/dry feet policy. The policy is a result of several years of jockeying between the Cuban and US governments to determine a mutually agreeable manner of handling interdictions while maintaining a refugee policy. The basic approach is if Cubans successfully make landfall on US soil, they can apply for asylee status, but if they are intercepted by sea, they are returned to Cuba. Several scenarios have challenged this seemingly arbitrary designation but the most famous is the case of Elián González. Interdicted at sea after his boat capsized, with the death of most on board, including his mother, a custody battle erupted between his father in Cuba and his mother's family in Miami. The resulting media fervor over the case raised the ire of anti-Cuban, anti-Cuban American, pro-Castro, and anti-Castro forces alike. The case was resolved when US 11th Circuit Court of Appeals ordered the boy returned to his father, but the media images most associated with the case were armed Border Patrol agents wrestling him away from the closet of a relatives' home in Little Havana. The reality is a punitive immigration system that denies access to citizenship and creates the very forms of political and economic marginalization it tends to blame on the immigrants themselves.

The final act of criminalization, the *fait accompli*, was introduced by Wisconsin Republican representative James Sensenbrenner and passed by Congress in 2005 to make being undocumented, or assisting an undocumented immigrant, a felony crime. The Sensenbrenner Bill HR 4437 passed the House by a vote of 239 to 182 but was not reconciled with a stalled Senate immigration bill before any of its measures were enacted into law. The bill emboldened Republican representatives to present bills that would have called for mass deportations of "illegals." Independent journalist David Bacon was one of the first to expose Sensenbrenner's business connections, as a family heir to the Kimberly Clark fortune, and the corporation's total reliance on Latino immigrant laborers. The forestry industry is increasingly dependent upon H-2B temporary visa holders and Kimberly Clark, as the largest supplier of paper products (from Kleenex tissue to Kotex tampons), relies upon immigrant tree cutters to provide the necessary pulp. "Every year, laborers from Mexico, Central America, and the Caribbean are recruited for this job. In towns like La Democracia, Guatemala, where the global fall in coffee prices has driven families to the edge of hunger, recruiters promise jobs paying more in an hour than a coffee farmer can make in a day. . . . But in the United States and other wealthy countries, economic rights are not considered human rights. In this official view, hunger doesn't create political refugees" (Bacon 2008: 66–8). The political ramifications of designating immigrants' motivation in either economic or political terms are clearly displayed in the underlying motive of making unauthorized border-crossing a felony. It guarantees a steady supply of the cheapest, most marginalized, and exploited labor that capital can secure itself with the power of the state.

To denounce Sensenbrenner's 4437, some of the largest demonstrations in the history of the nation were organized in most major cities to support immigrant rights. The response to criminalization was resounding and launched what became the largest protest movement since the anti-Vietnam War era. The next chapter begins with the immigrant rights movement when considering the fourth form of citizenship – cultural citizenship.

4

Cultural Citizenship, Gender, and Labor

When the immigrant rights movement marched onto the national scene in the spring of 2006, organizing efforts were spearheaded by labor unions committed to representing immigrants. The timing of Sensenbrenner's Bill and the existing network of immigrant advocacy organizations put these two converging forces together for one of the largest demonstrations in American history. The immigrant rights movement and their collective call to stand up, speak out, and come out of the shadows of the law and society constitutes exactly what Leo Chavez (2008: 161) describes as claims on cultural citizenship. "Although legal status and nativist attitudes may make inclusion of immigrants into society problematic, the marchers, with their US flags in full display, were making a statement about their sense of belonging and their social and cultural citizenship." One of the most important unions responsible for getting immigrants and their supporters on the streets for the protests was the United Farm Workers (UFW).

In many respects, Christine Chávez Delgado was born to be a union organizer. Since birth, Chávez Delgado was surrounded by the bustling activity of the National Farm Workers Association (NFWA), a precursor union to the UFW that her grandfather, César Chávez, helped to found in 1962 when the plight of agricultural workers drew little support from the US public, and even less from organized labor. Throughout her childhood, Chávez Delgado bore witness to significant changes in the US Latino population and in labor organizing strategies that would fundamentally alter the direction of the American labor movement a few decades later. At the age of four, Chávez Delgado was arrested along with her parents in Detroit, Michigan, during the table grape and lettuce strike or *huelga*, which began in 1965 and ended in 1970. Chávez Delgado's childhood experience was a common one among children of agricultural workers, who, with family members, struggled for better workplace conditions. The five-year grape and lettuce strike, which came at a heavy cost to many, also paid off immeasurably for most: agricultural workers negotiated a labor contract with growers through collective bargaining procedures while the needs of women and children were addressed as part of the core concerns of farmworkers.

Beyond the formal recognition of political citizenship (i.e., pathways to naturalization and attendant access to full rights, status, and identity), "Cultural citizenship attends, not only to dominant exclusions and marginalizations, but also to subordinate aspirations for and definitions of enfranchisement" (Rosaldo 1997: 37). Latino immigrants, by transcending their marginalized citizenship status, are enacting forms of cultural citizenship to strive for empowerment, solidarity and community building, self-definition, and anti-subordination struggles. Often operating outside the legal channels afforded to rights-bearing citizens, claims are nonetheless made in the demand for *respeto* (or respect), space, and autonomy. "Cultural citizenship offers the possibility of legitimizing demands made in the struggle to enfranchise themselves. These demands can range from political and economic issues to matters of human dignity, well-being and respect" (Rosaldo 1994: 57).

It is the intersections of gender relations, labor organizing, and cultural citizenship that we explore in this chapter. The early history of Mexican labor organizing, often with women at the forefront, informs the UFW's struggle for gender egalitarianism and equal representation. Additionally, recent immigrant labor organizing struggles feed into the current immigrant rights movement. These struggles at the crossroads of time and space are key in the making of Latinos' quintessentially American rights claims – traversing the well-worn paths paved by abolitionists, suffragettes, civil rights activists, feminists, and labor organizers.

Among Latino and Latina workers, cultural citizenship operates within a political terrain of multiple inequalities based on gender, class, race, and national origin. Latinas, in particular, have been catalysts for creating social change that emerge from everyday practices of working in menial jobs without any protection or guarantees. For them, the meaning of cultural citizenship encompasses their home, workplace, and community. Latina workers utilize extended family and work-based networks to fight against repressive labor conditions while expanding their personal rights as wives, mothers, domestic partners, and daughters (Segura and Pierce 1993). Latina workers are among the most prominent union leaders, who have unified native-born, immigrant, and working-class workers. Their labor organizing successes today, however, follow in a long line of Latina labor activists who have struggled for civic and social belonging in decades prior.

Labor Organizing and the Origins of Latina/o Inclusion

Early labor organizing successes came at a time when immigration was waning and working folks were reeling from unprecedented levels of economic despair. In 1935, the National Labor Relations Act rolled out on the heels of the mass repatriation of millions of Mexicans immigrants and US citizens of Mexican descent. The right to collective bargaining, or joining a union, was restricted to citizens only, yet it was a dissident group of naturalized immigrants, these notable women organizers, who were key to crossing the lines of nation, race, class, and gender to spawn the union movement.

Due to the social isolation Mexicans endured in the United States, many actively formed self-help groups to provide a "broad range of benefits and services [that] they otherwise could not afford" (Gutiérrez 1995: 34). *Mutualistas* promoted Mexican culture with concrete assistance such as loans, death benefits, financial assistance, bilingual schools, and even served as insurance providers for the poor (Acuña 2010: 78, 196; Hernández

1983). These groups were especially important during the Great Depression. For instance, due to their status as second-class citizens, many Mexican Americans were fired from their jobs and replaced by whites. During this time of "widespread poverty" many Mexican communities set up cooperatives that sold *tamales*[9] at cost to help feed unemployed and hungry families – they sold, not gave, the food because despite being "on the brink of starvation" many Mexicans "considered taking welfare almost worse" (Acuña 2010: 219). Specific mutual aid societies included *La Alianza Hispano Americana, La Hermandad Mexicana Nacional, Sociedad Progresista Mexicana, La Orden de Caballeros de Honor, Sociedad Mutualista Masonica Benito Juarez, Sociedad Mutualista Miguel Hidalgo, Sociedad Mutualista Ignacia Zaragosa,* and the *Sociedad Mutualista de Beneficiencia de Señoras y Señoritas* (García 1989; Hernández 1983).[10] The history of these self-help groups reveals the roots of the type of community unionism adopted later by the UFW and furthered in the Justice for Janitors (J4J) organizing campaigns that directly focused on improving the lives of Latina/o immigrants.

By the mid-1930s, Mexican workers, which included entire families with children, were a mainstay in American agriculture and manufacturing. The Mexican-born population living in the United States had more than doubled, from 220,000 in 1910 to 478,000 in 1920 (Gutiérrez 1995: 45). Mexican immigrants filled a range of occupational niches, especially in mining, agriculture, and railroad construction. By the end of the decade, Mexican immigrant laborers populated cities like Chicago, Los Angeles, Detroit, and San Antonio and worked in the garment, canning, automobile, and pecan-shelling industries. Although more established Latino communities had some middle-class families, most Latinos were of working-class status who occupied both agricultural and industrial-sector jobs, the former with greater preponderance.

The origins of the Latino labor movement are evidenced by one particular *mutualista* and its work on behalf of Mexican immigrants and Mexican Americans laboring in the mining industry. No other organization matched the size and geographic reach of *La Alianza Hispano Americana.* Beginning in Tucson, Arizona, as a fraternal organization serving its Mexican middle- and upper-class leaders, *La Alianza* became prominent in California, Arizona, New Mexico, and Texas. There were chapters formed in at least nine Mexican states as well. Orozco (1995: 12) notes that women in *La Alianza* were extended full membership after 1913 but women's membership was restricted to the ladies auxiliary from 1894 to 1913:

> Although the founders and early organizers of the Alianza Hispano Americana were men of wealth, education, and high standing, the majority of its members were of humble origin, belonging to the Mexican-American laboring class. The organization dealt principally with the various problems of the working class. In areas where labor unions were unable to hurdle the many obstacles placed before them, the Alianza assumed the function of a workingmen's union, persuading Mexican American workers to come forward and challenge the managers of capital for better working conditions and fair wage increases. On June 1, 1903, for instance, Mexican American miners were active participants in the Clifton-Morenci district strike.... Between 1,200 and 1,500 striking workers, 80 to 90 percent of whom were miners of Mexican descent, armed themselves and took control of the mines, compelling the companies to shut down their operations. (Hernández 1983: 35–6)

At the time leading up to the *Alianza*-supported strike, Mexican miners were paid $2.50 for a ten-hour day while Anglo miners earned $3.50 (Hernández 1983: 37). The strike centered around three central grievances: (1) better pay and fewer hours, (2) improved working and living conditions such as medical access and company store price reductions, and (3) recognition. The idea of recognition centered on miners' wish to be considered as a viable union of workers with grievances to be collectively resolved. Unfortunately, the strike faltered on all three counts when a freak storm and flash flood nearly washed away the town. Secondly, with the help of a militia deputized by local sheriffs and the US Army detachment that was dispatched to protect mining company interests, the company broke the line and forced miners back to jobs with reduced hours and significantly reduced wages.

The mining industry was traditionally one of the most dangerous and underpaid sectors of the US economy. Yet, the deplorable working conditions were not passively accepted by Mexican miners. Some of the most important pushes for labor organizing in the Southwest came directly out of the struggle to end the dual wage structure, to improve the living conditions in the company towns, and to unite white ethnics, Mexican Americans, Mexican immigrants, Asian Americans, and Blacks in the class struggle against large mining companies. Concessions were not easily exacted and the full-scale suppression of labor organization and mass protest became the definitive response of mining companies to workers' demands.

One of the most effective ways of discrediting the labor movement in the mining industry was to link it with the anti-communist sentiment of the Cold War era. Chicano historian Mario T. García (1989) notes that labor organizing by smelter workers in the El Paso–Cuidad Juarez border region was characterized by companies and local law enforcement as communist inspired. No better way is this represented than in the events leading up to and the eventual production of the International Union of Mine, Mill, and Smelter Workers sponsored film, *Salt of the Earth*. The Empire Zinc Company, a subsidiary of the largest zinc company in the United States, owned a company town and mines in Grant County, New Mexico. In 1950, the miners voted to strike for an end to the dual wage structure and better working conditions. A series of injunctions barred the male workers from striking but the resourcefulness of the community brought women from Ladies Auxiliary Local 209 onto the picket line. As Mine-Mill union organizer, and later co-star in the film, Clinton Jencks observed:

> One, it was an all-male industry. None of these women were working actually on the job . . . their whole lives were involved, but who thinks about women that are in the home. They're only struggling to stretch the paycheck. They're only doing, you know. *Only* . . . and that [is] the way we've been used to thinking. . . . So when this explosion comes . . . the women taking over is the thing that excited the imagination of people all over. (cited in Lorence 1999: 30)

What attracted three blacklisted Hollywood filmmakers to this saga of Mexican American women on the picket lines in support of their Mine-Mill partners certainly was the larger story of vast racial, class, and gender inequalities in capitalist America. The film cast included a number of the members of Mine-Mill Local 890, Ladies Auxiliary 209, and Mexican actress Rosaura Revueltas. However, the film never found its way into US cinema distribution as it was blocked by not only the conservative projectionist union but the House Committee on Un-American Activities (HUAC) and the US Intelligence Agency. *Salt of the Earth* became better known as the only blacklisted film in US history rather than the story of the Mine-Mill strike by Mexican and Anglo mining families protesting for better working and living conditions.

The film captured the grassroots activism and gender egalitarianism, often initiated in *mutualistas*, which propelled Mexican immigrant and Mexican American women into union leadership as officers and rank-and-file organizers. In 1938, Emma Tenayuca, at the age of 22, was already considered to be one of the most effective union organizers in the country. For her fiery speeches and keen organizing skills, Tenayuca was appointed the secretary general for the Workers' Alliance of America, a union with ties to the Texas Communist Party, in which she was also a member. In San Antonio, Texas, the young Tenayuca rallied more than 10,000 pecan-shellers, 90 percent of whom were Mexican women and among the city's poorest residents, to strike for higher wages and better working conditions. At that time, malnutrition, the nation's highest infant mortality rate, and endemic tuberculosis plagued West San Antonio, a high-density, poverty-stricken neighborhood. In 1934, the wages of the shellers averaged $1.00–$4.00 a week, or $192 annually. Although national minimum wage standards were not yet established, four years later in 1938 when a benchmark was recognized, workers earned $15.60 a week, or $810 annually (Vargas 1997: 565). Pecan-shellers earned less than one-quarter of the minimum wage, the lowest wages in the nation, and that forced families to draw on the labor of their children. A Mexican family working together could earn 5–6 cents per pound for shelled pecans, but in actuality most made less because payment of wages often depended on the quality of the nuts cracked: whole nuts paid more than broken halves while nut fragments paid nothing. Under these conditions, the mostly-Latina workforce walked out of their jobs in 1938 and demanded three concessions: restoration of wages to the point prior to a recent cut, an end to illegal homework, and remediation of poor working conditions. Drawing on family networks and self-help organizations or *mutualistas*, the pecan-shellers' walkout resulted in the temporary shutdown of their workplace.

Even though Tenayuca was arrested on charges of communist agitation, the pecan-shellers persisted in their strike activity. Workers held meetings in West San Antonio neighborhoods to organize a strike against the employer, the Southern Pecan Shelling Company. Women formed the majority of strikers, just as they comprised a significant proportion of the Workers' Alliance membership. The strike brought many women out of their homes and into the streets for the first time. Adapting to their new role as strikers, they persuaded their husbands and children to come to the rallies, where they could also be educated about the issues. After 37 days of strike activity, the pecan-shellers successfully forced the owners to raise their pay to 0.25 cents an hour, although the average annual income of pecan-shellers' families remained abysmally low. According to historian Rodolfo Acuña (2010), the annual income for a pecan-shellers' family comprised of four to six persons was $251. The pecan-shellers' strike is considered by many historians to be the first significant victory in the Mexican American struggle for political and economic equality, and most importantly, women led the way.

Similarly, the origins of the more militant, racially inclusive Congress of Industrial Organizations (CIO) can be partially credited to the organizing tactics and leadership skills of another Latina union organizer – Luisa Moreno. Her labor organizing efforts spanned the United States from the garment shops of New York City to the cigar plants in Tampa and the canneries in Los Angeles. Moreno, an immigrant from Guatemala, was the first Latina vice president of the United Cannery, Agricultural,

Packing, and Allied Workers of America (UCAPAWA), a union that helped to form the CIO along with the United Mine Workers, Mine-Mill (IUMMSW), and the International Ladies' Garment Workers' Union (ILGWU) to name the unions with a prominent Latino presence. In Los Angeles during the late 1930s, Moreno organized a walkout of 430 workers at the California Sanitary Canning Company (Cal San). Under Moreno's leadership, the mostly Mexican and Russian Jewish female workforce fought for the recognition of their union – the Local 75 of UCAPAWA – and a closed shop, or a form of union security in which the employer agrees to only hire union members. By securing the recognition of UCAPAWA, Cal San management would be man-dated to work with the union for the betterment of its members, that is, the workers at Cal San. Moreno, through kin networks, organized the walkout. Sisters, mothers, cousins, uncles, and aunts worked together for union recognition, drawing on a sense of common purpose and family ties. In 1940, UCAPAWA was recognized by Cal San and other food-processing plants as the official representative of cannery workers and a closed shop. The philosophy of placing women at the leadership of the union per-sisted as UCAPAWA recruited women from shop stewards to vice presidents (Ruiz 1987: 38).

Importantly, the activism of Moreno, Tenayuca, and other Latinas aimed for change beyond the confines of their union. *El Congreso del Pueblo de Habla Española* (the Spanish-Speaking Congress) was one of the first organized attempts to bring together the mutual aid society framework, labor organizations, and popular front politics. Organized by Luisa Moreno, *El Congreso* formed chapters throughout the Southwest under the operating framework: "For an alliance between the Spanish speaking people and the progressive, all democratic forces among the Anglo-American and minority groups in the United States on behalf of the preservation and extension of American democratic institutions" (García 1989: 147). The organization boasted over 2 million members, and in their 1938 conference, held in Los Angeles, del-egates endorsed a platform addressing jobs, access to agricultural lands, housing, health, education, discrimination, unlawful deportations, and youth-related issues (García 1989: 148). Quality of life concerns were considered equal to stock union concerns such as collective bargaining, wage gains, working conditions, and full employment. Organizations such as *El Congreso* initiated the community unionism approach, to be adopted later by the United Farm Workers and the SEIU's (Service Employees International Union) Justice for Janitors campaign.

Though short-lived, *El Congreso* brought together varied constituencies from farmworker advocates such as Josefina Fierro de Bright, Communist Party and labor organizers such as Emma Tenayuca, then-International Longshoremen's and Warehousemen's Union (ILWU) organizer Bert Corona, and public intellectuals like Carey McWilliams, Paul S. Taylor, Arthur Campa, and George I. Sanchez. Members hailed from California, Texas, Arizona, New Mexico, Colorado, and even the Midwest and Florida. World War II squashed the hopes and organization of *El Congreso* but in many ways its last stand took place in 1942 with the formation of the Sleepy Lagoon Defense Committee. Organized by Josefina Fierro de Bright and including lawyer Carey McWilliams and organizer Bert Corona, the committee defended the legal rights of 24 Mexican youth who were framed on murder charges. As Denning (1998: 18) notes: "the two years of the defense campaign coincided with a moral panic about 'Mexican crime' that swept Southern California, culminating in the 'zoot suit' race riots of June 1943." The wartime racialization of Mexican youth allowed a murder trial to take place where stereotypes of pack animal-like Chicano street gangs were entered as evidence while Navy servicemen, with impunity, summarily beat and harassed Chicano street youth who wore the fashionable zoot suits. The remnants of the Chicana/o Popular Front were the very last line of defense for criminalized, racialized Mexican-origin youth and once the violence subsided, the activists were met with red-baiting and government-sponsored programs that deported political dissidents on trumped up immigration infractions (both Moreno and Fierro de Bright were deported in addition to several other Mexican leftist activists).

Community Unionism, Gender Parity, and the United Farm Workers

By the time Christine Chávez Delgado joined the UFW as its political director in 2005, hers was among several unions with female-led and community-based approaches to organizing workers. Unions with leadership and philosophical approaches similar to the UFW, Workers' Alliance, and UCAPAWA, in fact, grew in numbers and effectiveness beginning in the 1980s and continue to increase in membership and success to the present day. These unions (e.g., UFW, SEIU, and UNITE-HERE) are the only sector of organized labor that is actually growing in membership as overall union participation rates are declining precipitously. The Change-to-Win Federation split from the AFL-CIO in 2005, with the UFW adopting to affiliate with both federations, over precisely this issue of how best to rebuild the union movement. Yet, the origins of the most widely recognized union representing predominately Latino farmworkers is rooted in the charisma of César Chávez but equally connected to the prominent role of women in UFW leadership roles.

When Dolores Huerta organized farmworkers in the California fields, she drew on the labor mobilization strategies of her Latina predecessors. Huerta looked to women to articulate their needs as workers, mothers, and members of society. As a mother of 11 children and the UFW's principal labor contract negotiator, Huerta continued the strategies of placing the individual, family, and community needs at the center of the farmworker agenda. Huerta's close relationship with César Chávez afforded the activist a direct position to observe, comment, and make recommendations for farmworkers. "In Michigan, the farmworker children there are ashamed to say that they're farmworkers or that their parents are farmworkers. That's got to end. We have to get farmworkers the same types of benefits, the same type of wages, the respect that they deserve because they do the most sacred work of all. They feed our nation every day" (Huerta 2008: 185). Poverty, social injustice, and exploitation propelled Huerta to directly lobby legislators and growers for social change. In a 1990 interview, she articulated her motivation, "To me, racism, chauvinism, is part of the air you breathe, the water you drink. It surrounds you, so you have to learn how to fight it, deal with it work in spite of it. You can't let it get you down or paralyze you. You have to do all you can to change it" (Huerta 2008: 279). Her activist beginnings were rooted in the co-founding of Stockton's Community Service Organization (CSO), where she met fellow organizer Chávez, and together they would launch the most recognized Latino union in history.

Jessica Govea came to the farmworkers' movement in a similar fashion. Her parents began the Bakersfield chapter of the CSO and when she came of age, she joined CSO veterans Fred Ross, César Chávez, and Dolores Huerta in the struggle for farmworker rights:

> When I was seven, a man came and knocked on our door. That visit – from Fred Ross, at the time working with Saul Alinsky's Industrial Areas Foundation and the principle organizer of the Community Service Organization, marked an important point in the course my life has taken. CSO was founded in East Los Angeles in the late 1940's by young Chicano WWII veterans and industrial union activists who weren't prepared to continue accepting things as they were after serving on the front lines of both the war and labor organizing. (Govea 2000)

Eventually, Govea would lead grape boycott campaigns (at times single handedly) in Montreal and Toronto to eventually become the UFW National Director of Organizing. After internal dissension within UFW ranks led to a purge, she shifted her efforts to assisting the coffee-processing workers' union in El Salvador during the nation's civil war. In the 2000 speech she gave while working on a book never finished due to losing her battle with cancer at the age of 58, a battle she attributed to prolonged pesticide exposure, she stated most perceptively: "I write for those who are visible enough to be disrespected and invisible enough to be dismissed."

Against seemingly insurmountable odds, the UFW came to represent a larger struggle on the part of a racialized and economically marginalized Mexican American population. Nowhere were Mexican Americans more marginalized than in the fields as migrant workers. Every time the UFW registered a win against wealthy Anglo growers, the "*si se puede*" or "yes we can" rally cry or *grito* was a call to all Mexican American activists who saw their struggles as intertwined with the farmworker struggle.

Recently, two expositions of the UFW were published by *Los Angeles Times* reporter Miriam Pawel and Tenderloin Housing Clinic Director Randy Shaw. One a harsh indictment, the other a celebration of accomplishments past and present, both wistful that the sun has set on the UFW, yet divided on how the long shadow of the UFW's history should be defined as either singularly controversial or inspirational. Pawel (2009) begins with the leadership purge and traces history back to show how César Chávez's iron grip over the union led to his unwillingness to deal with contrarian views and subsequently unraveled the union, whereas Shaw (2008) starts with the UFW accomplishments of achieving the seemingly impossible and how an entire generation of organizers cut their teeth on the UFW and now lead some of today's most successful labor unions and organizing campaigns among Latino immigrant workers.

Both are slightly exaggerated accounts and somewhere in between the two lies the truth, but the legacy of the UFW, out of the purge, points to some of the most important leaders in today's labor movement. Similar to how McAdam (1990) identified the significance of the 1964 Freedom Summer as the catalyst for subsequent civil rights, women's rights, anti-war, and free speech movements, the UFW has given rise to the new union and immigrant rights movements. In the summer of '64, the Student Nonviolent Coordinating Committee brought northern college students to Mississippi to assist in voter registration campaigns and freedom schools for African American children, and the events transformed a generation that would lead most subsequent 1960s protest movements. Shaw (2008) contends that the UFW strikes and boycotts are directly responsible for initially training and inspiring the current organizers who are now shaping this era of immigrant rights, labor struggle, and cultural citizenship.

Nowhere is this on fuller display than the Justice for Janitors campaign and the Immigrant Workers Freedom Rides of 2003.

Justice for Janitors

Shaw (2008) notes that the largest beneficiary of the UFW's downfall is the Service Employees International Union (SEIU), currently the second largest labor union with 2.2 million members and one of the few unions that is actually growing in a climate of rapidly dwindling unionization rates. The Justice for Janitors (J4J) movement is known for incorporating entire families, making women's mothering roles as public as their roles as laborers (Cranford 1998). By creating a family atmosphere, the movement has taken away conflicts between motherhood and organizing by ensuring both family and the union are responsible for children. This breaks down gendered role expectations and allows women to walk side by side with men to fight for rights, ultimately expecting them to receive those same rights. Women, alongside men, fought for the betterment of themselves and their families. With the help of the SEIU, a well-established labor union with then over 2 million members nationwide and in Canada, in 1985, the J4J began mobilizing janitors in Denver, Colorado, under the leadership of Stephen Lerner. With Lerner at the helm, the J4J employed the tactics he learned from the UFW such as evoking imagery of worker exploitation, staging hunger strikes and vigils, performing street drama, and blocking traffic. Importantly, the J4J's strategy of "community unionism" placed Latina immigrant workers, who made up just over half of the janitorial workforce, as crucial actors in the labor movement. The recent wins for janitors at the University of Miami and in the high-rises of downtown Houston show the real strength of the SEIU as one of the few unions prepared for collective bargaining in a post-industrial economy.

In 1988, when the campaign moved to Los Angeles, California, the J4J campaign gained much-needed momentum from direct action strategies employed by strike leaders and members of the rank-and-file. Although the SEIU was a strong union among other workers in other areas of the labor market in Canada and the United States, by the mid-1980s, membership in the SEIU Local 399 in Los Angeles dropped 77 percent, and the SEIU represented only 8 percent of janitors in Los Angeles or approximately 1,500 workers (Acuña 1996: 185). In 1983, an average janitor working in Los Angeles earned just over $7.00 an hour. Full healthcare insurance was also extended to the janitor and the janitor's family members. Three years later, things shifted dramatically: by 1986, wages were reduced to $4.50 an hour and healthcare benefits were not extended. Attempts to organize workers were ineffective, and some observed, outdated for the workplace conditions and the labor force (Acuña 1996; Cranford 1998). In the early 1980s, the SEIU Local 399 attempted to organize janitors drawing on established NLRB (National Labor Relations Board) strategies for organizing. Workplace-based elections for union recognition were held at open-shop buildings, but in the end, too few workers were organized and cleaning companies retaliated against the union drives by hiring non-union labor.

The new campaign, which drew on direct action, street theater, rank-and-file organizing, bilingualism, and community support, infused workers with a sense of solidarity and substantive organizing skills to mount a successful campaign for better workplace conditions and higher wages. Significantly, the SEIU did not call for a strike, gauging accurately that the workers would be readily replaced by others who would be available and willing to work for even lower pay and fewer benefits. Jono Shaffer, a college graduate and experienced grassroots organizer, Rocío Sáenz, a Mexico City-born, former university student, along with rank-and-file members Bertha Northey, Ana Navarette, and Patricia Recino, placed the needs of families, workers, and women at the center of the SEIU's organizing agenda. Together, Shaffer, Sáenz, Northey, Navarette, and Recino increased union membership by adapting grassroots techniques and gendered strategies of organizing that were unique to the Los Angeles worker landscape.

Century City, a wealthy Los Angeles neighborhood abutting Beverly Hills, was the first arena of political action for the J4J. The dual-shop practices of Century Cleaning were labor organizing fodder for the Local 399. Rather than viewing the dual-shop as a barrier to unionizing laborers, the J4J began a mobilization drive in Century City applying new tactics of labor organizing. A few important elements characterize this new wave of labor organizing. The first element seeks union recognition and neutrality agreements eschewing elections monitored by the NLRB for direct pressure. Secondly, the union drives consist of intensive rank-and-file campaigns in which union members volunteer to organize unorganized workers. Because of the concentration of women, immigrants, and ethnic groups in most low-wage, service sector jobs, involvement of workers also helped to diversify the mostly male, white leadership of union organizing drives. An ethnically diverse leadership cohort is crucial because it aids in recruiting not only non-union workers but community allies as well. Coalitions between unions are the fourth element of this wave of labor organizing, and alliances with religious and community groups are the fifth. Significantly, religious and community groups do not fall under restrictions of US labor law prohibiting action (such as picketing) against secondary employers. The sixth element is wage campaigns in the court of public opinion so that they captivate the public and hearken back to popular labor movements of old (Banks 1991). J4J organizers understood all too well that in order to secure union recognition they needed to appeal to a sense of justice that resonated with the public at large. To counter the replacement of striking workers, which was legal and practiced widely, the J4J mobilized community support, often drawing on the clergy and high-profile personalities.

Coupled with later successes in organizing Silicon Valley and Sacramento high-rise janitors, the California janitorial organizing model has been replicated at the University of Miami and downtown Houston. Both Florida and Texas are right-to-work states, and both pose particular challenges to organizing campaigns, but the SEIU has followed the leadership of executive vice president and UFW alum Eliseo Medina and forged ahead with one of the most ambitious organizing strategies to date.

At the University of Miami, the SEIU has taken on Boston-based contractor UNICCO Services by targeting the absentee company and University of Miami president Donna Shalala (a former Clinton cabinet member) and staging a series of civil disobedience acts including a hunger strike, sit-ins, marches, and building coalitions and support from student, church, and community groups to place the plight of the poverty-waged janitors onto the national media stage. Vice president Medina joined the janitors in a hunger strike that resulted in the hospitalization of several strikers. The organizing campaign, led by the same Lerner who started J4J in Denver, broadened the Latino base of janitors to include primarily Cuban refugee women into the ranks of the SEIU. "Maritza Paz, who was admitted to the United States 13 years ago as a political refugee from Cuba, hired on at the university 11 years ago at $4.35 an hour. When the strike began, she had worked her way up to a sumptuous $6.70 hourly wage with no benefits, for which she cleaned 17 bathrooms and 20 offices every day" (Meyerson 2006: A23). The university relented on May 1, 2006 when it agreed to require its contractor UNICCO to allow majority union elections and thus bargain with the SEIU. "The contract, which runs from Sept. 1, 2006 through Aug. 31, 2010, provides janitors with raises each year, and guarantees that their health care will remain affordable" (http://yeswecane.org, accessed May 5, 2010). As much as this was a labor organizing campaign, quotes from striking workers point to the central demands being nearly always couched in terms of cultural citizenship (respect, dignity, and recognition):

> Reinaldo Hernandez stated, "the money is needed, what we want is dignity and respect."

> A fasting Feliciano Hernandez attested, "They are treating us like dogs. We can't allow this to continue."

> Clara Vargas stated she "never imagined janitors in Miami would have so much support, but now we know the world is watching and our voices are being heard." (Shaw 2008: 111, 112, 114)

The campaign to organize Houston janitors has taken on a similar cast. Large displays of public theater (together with a well-financed national advertising campaign) holding oil conglomerates like

Chevron responsible for employing janitors at poverty-level wages, were coupled with direct action tactics on the ground that featured the lives of hard-working, poorly remunerated Latina immigrants as the rallying point. "The janitors who organized in Houston represented four of the five largest cleaning companies in the city and the companies agreed to allow the union to try to organize their employees. That agreement [representing 5,300 workers] came after the union organized a 10-day strike by Houston janitors" (Gamboa 2006). An estimated 80 protestors engaged in acts of civil disobedience even though firings and arrests were constantly threatened. On November 16, 2006, mounted police charged 50 Houston janitors and supporters during non-violent protest and this action seemed to turn public support squarely in favor of the striking janitors. As Medina (cited in Gamboa 2006) has described the SEIU Justice for Janitors strategy,

> "I think we've shown that workers in the campaign in the South and Southwest want to be organized and need to be organized and if unions come forth with a plan and a vision, workers will answer the call," said Medina who spoke to a group of reporters. All but two of the 17 states, New Mexico and Colorado, are right-to-work states, meaning workers in those states always have the right to decide whether to join a union. Union membership in all the states, except Nevada, is between 2 percent and 4 percent, Medina said. Nevada's is about 14 percent, largely because of the gaming industry there, he said.

The union is attempting to add to its 2.2 million member base with its immigrant organizing attempts in the Southwest and southern United States. It all began in Los Angeles and Century City with the highly recognizable J4J campaign but the SEIU has the potential to change the low-pay, no benefits service sector nationwide.

UNITE-HERE and New Labor's Ascendancy

US unions were historically tied to the manufacturing-based economy nation and the shift to service sector employment saw rates of deunionization soar. By 1985, membership in unions had declined to just 17 percent of the total workforce and current estimates of unionization identify 12 percent of total workforce and 8 percent of the private sector are union members. Efforts to reverse the deunionization trend are currently led by Latina labor organizers. They recognize Latinas are disproportionately represented in the "care" industries of the economy working as childcare workers, nannies, dry-cleaners, and house cleaners. As UNITE-HERE sought to organize garment workers, hotel workers, and fabricators (from muffler shops to tombstone producers), it was less about the job description and more about, as organizer Cristina Vasquez states, "building a union of immigrant workers . . . than a garment workers' union." Women's paid labor still closely follows the traditional roles of women within the home, such as the garment and cleaning industries, which pushes women into their traditionally defined female roles in society. Registered nurses, secretaries, housekeepers, and receptionists remain over 94.5 percent female.

UNITE-HERE's predecessors – the Hotel Employees and Restaurant Employees, which was established in 1891, the International Ladies' Garment Workers' Union, formed in 1900, and the Amalgamated Clothing Workers of America, formed in 1914 – combined into one union in 1995. Before this merger, both the International Ladies' Garment Workers' Union (ILGWU) and the Amalgamated Clothing and Textile Workers Union (ACTWU) – as it was then named – were struggling for both numbers and morale. At one point the two competitor unions could claim 900,000 members between them, but in 1995 that number had dropped to only 350,000 (McClure 1995). In order to save their organizing efforts the two unions decided to merge and form a new union, the Union of Needletrades, Industrial, and Textile Employees (UNITE). UNITE at its origin was created to focus on Central Americans and communicate with unions in Central America, Mexico, and the Caribbean, where many of these jobs were being outsourced.

The other half is one of the best examples of the inclusion of a Latina population, the Hotel Employees and Restaurant

Employees (HERE). Within the last 50 years, this industry has transformed from predominantly white, native-born employees to overwhelmingly immigrant and minority, including both Latino and Asian immigrant populations. These hotel jobs are considered extremely desirable by these immigrants, which leads to their commitment to these specific jobs and often leads to union involvement. Hotel managers also tend to underestimate the amount of education and social class held by these immigrants in their home nation. Holding positions in the middle class in their native lands often makes immigrants more likely to speak out. In order to use this powerful force of immigrant laborers, union contracts began to change in order to help documented and undocumented immigrants and especially promote women's concerns. These include extended leaves to visit relatives still in the native country, protection in case of changes in names and social security numbers, immigrant clauses in benefit packages, seeking multilingual approaches in management positions as an asset, and educational funds to improve workers' English. HERE is pressing outside traditional boundaries to use immigrant enthusiasm to add to the strength of the union, while helping this population gain equality in the greater US workforce.

In Los Angeles, the daughter of farmworkers rose up through the ranks of HERE to eventually take on the leadership of Local 11 and sit on the international board as an executive vice president. Maria Elena Durazo, and her late husband Miguel Contreras, have successively held the highest post of executive secretary of the LA County Federation of Labor since 1996. A growing union that successfully targets some of the largest hotel chains in major tourist and convention destinations worldwide, UNITE-HERE is both fiscally solvent and committed to organizing. Yet, it was Durazo who was instrumental in linking civil rights to cultural citizenship as the national director of the Immigrant Workers Freedom Rides of 2003. The precursor to the massive protests in 2006, Change-to-Win unions like UNITE-HERE and the SEIU were at the forefront of organizing immigrants in their demand for inclusion, amnesty, and respect:

Through the [HERE] union, immigrant workers are organizing to make hotel service jobs good jobs that all members of our community have a chance to fill. Throughout the Freedom Ride many union leaders had to confront anti-immigrant attitudes within their own ranks. I am sure you have heard the jargon and stereotypes regarding immigrants taking jobs. It was quite impressive to see that union leaders were stepping up and taking the heat to defend the rights of immigrants. (Durazo 2005: 192)

The National Coalition for Dignity and Amnesty is comprised of labor unions, church organizations, civil rights organizations, immigrant rights organizations, community-based organizations, and elected officials. Together, they coordinated, with Durazo and HERE's assistance, the Freedom Rides connecting the struggles of undocumented immigrants with the struggle against racial segregation of blacks in the South during the Civil Rights movement. The most prominent labor unions who have been working to organize the undocumented (SEIU, UNITE-HERE, UFW, and UFCW) sponsored, along with original Freedom Ride organizers and national immigrant advocacy organizations, nine buses in their journey to Queens, New York for a rally in support of a blanket amnesty program. The Freedom Riders were successful in publicizing their plight in local newspapers as they criss-crossed the nation, but the hoped-for huge media event with strong national television coverage did not happen and changes in immigration law did not result in regularization.

Unfortunately, the coverage was three years too late, but in 2006 the terms of the debate were irrevocably shifted when immigrants made demands for inclusion and full recognition of their cultural citizenship, in direct opposition to the rising tide of neoliberal nativism that would never again gain currency without opposition. So clearly in response to the nativist sentiment that informed HR 4437, the 2006 marchers explicitly made rights claims by calling for full inclusion and recognition by seeking access to the rights accorded with US citizenship. What developed out of the movement was a strong call for "amnesty" to allow all immigrants experiencing some form of marginalizing non-citizen status to regularize their status or clear the pathway to full citizenship. The proverbial genie was out of the bottle and at the forefront of these citizenship claims were most often Latinas, who were building on a long history of labor organizing to directly confront discrimination.

Conclusion

In the 1980s, the last stand of Mexican American unions followed a pattern of Mexican American women striking to reclaim their rights to equality in the workplace, as working families and for the continued viability of their communities. Interestingly, the last major labor struggle involving Mexican miners in Arizona followed almost the same storyline as events dramatized in *Salt of the Earth*. Author Barbara Kingsolver has documented the events in her book *Holding the Line*, and she notes the role that female miners and women in Clifton-Morenci played in the last union stand against the Phelps Dodge Corporation. After mine employees were legally restrained from picketing, the women's auxiliary took the place of male and female workers to keep the strike going over a two-year period. Many scholars of labor studies view it as the strike that demonstrated the end of the New Deal supported labor movement. National Guard troops and military equipment such as Huey helicopters were brought out in defense of Phelps Dodge and the strike dwindled with the eventual decertification of the union. By 1980, the AFL and CIO had been combined for 25 years and even in their unity, the struggle for organized labor's very survival was at stake.

Since the 1980s assault on organized labor, today's unions have been required to adapt quickly to new workforces, labor relations, economic restructuring, and corporate/state opposition. Changes in the workforce and economic restructuring intensified an array of worker–management tensions in labor markets dominated by Latina and immigrant workers. The economic restructuring of the US economy was recognized when the events of the oil shock of 1973 unfolded and it became apparent there was a shift underway from a manufacturing-based economy to one based in the service sector. Industries in which workers produced or assembled goods from raw materials were relocated overseas. In 1965, manufacturing accounted for 53 percent of the US economy, but by 2004, comprised just 9 percent (*Benson's Economic and Market Trends* February 27, 2004). As a result, jobs in the service sector, which is characterized by a higher incidence of low-wage, low-skilled jobs where workers face formidable barriers to unionize, have increased significantly. At the same time, manufacturing production jobs which are characterized by higher wages, job securities, and membership in unions are much less common in the US labor sector.

Considering this new terrain that organized labor must traverse, Chávez Delgado alongside other Latina union pioneers has created substantial differences in the lives of many Latinas. In order to understand how these women's social relationships have changed with their persistence and desire to take up the leadership helms in unions, it is important to underscore that significant changes in workplace and household structures have reshaped women's relationship to the workplace and the home environment since the mid-twentieth century. Menjívar notes in her study of Central American immigrant women working in California: "The structure of opportunity for these immigrants is shaped by restrictive immigration policies that deny them security of residence and rights to work and by the dynamics of the local economy. [The situation of increased opportunities for paid work and higher earning power] does not automatically benefit women and sometimes ends up reinforcing gender subordination in families" (Menjívar 1997: 120).

For Latinas, the meaning of cultural citizenship encompasses their home, workplace, and community. Latina workers utilize extended family and work-based networks to fight against repressive labor conditions while expanding their personal rights as wives, mothers, domestic partners, and daughters (Segura and Pierce 1993). For those Latinas who are among the most prominent union leaders, they strive to unify native-born, immigrant, and working-class workers. Their labor organizing successes today, however, follow in a long line of Latina labor activists who have struggled for civic and social belonging in decades prior.

In the face of rising nativism and state controls, the immigrant rights movement, marked by the 2006 marches, demonstrates that enactments of and claims on cultural citizenship practices most often transcend national citizenship status. The marchers literally claimed their rightful space in the United States as flag-waving, peaceful protestors taking to the streets in the name of human rights. The mass media were forced to cover an alternative, new frame of representation. Immigrants would not be characterized as nameless, faceless hordes of criminals illegally crossing borders but families with children who were demanding the right to work, live, and contribute to the nation. "America also learned a bit more about the immigrants in their midst, those faceless folks who do much of the work cast aside by the educated and well-off among the citizenry. Suddenly those who lived shadowed lives were demonstrating in the open, in the reckless disregard of the practices of surveillance and laws of deportation governing their lives" (Chavez 2008: 174). Yet, claims on all forms of citizenship are much more complicated in an increasingly transnational context, the subject of the next chapter.

5

Transnational Identities

El Rey de Tomate, or the Tomato King, occupied two worlds in his 58 years of life on earth. Andrés Bermúdez Viramontes was born and raised in Jerez, Zacatecas, Mexico though he spent his entire married life in the United States, all the while working his way up the agricultural ladder.[11] He was fond of recounting the story of his marriage and the couple's swift decision in the early 1970s (the exact year varies in most accounts) to *van al norte* (migrate to the United States), which was facilitated by hiding in the trunk of a car to cross the Tijuana–San Diego border. Bermúdez found work in the agricultural fields near Sacramento and thus he began his married life as a farmworker in the tomato fields of the Central Valley. He quickly climbed to the position of crew boss, then reached the farm labor contractor rung, until he achieved the nearly impossible feat of buying land and joining the ranks of the grower class. Upon inventing an automated tomato planting machine, he attained riches rarely if ever attained by those locked in the system of agribusiness exploitation. The elevated status from grower to inventor attained by Bermúdez represents a true American Dream fulfilled – a modern-day Horatio Alger.

Yet in 2001, Bermúdez made history when he won a mayoral election in his Mexican hometown, making him the first immigrant residing in the United States to be elected to Mexican political office. Legal issues arose and eventually his appointment was negated due to his listing of Winters, California as his primary residence. When he ran his campaign, he offered his own transnational style of patronage politics, making the campaign promise that he would secure, in exchange for their vote, hundreds of H-2A temporary visas to *jerezanos* looking for work on his Winters, California farm (Bakker and Smith 2003). When Bermúdez passed away in 2009, the Jerez virtual community (www.jerez.com.mx) mourned the passing of a legend who won a second election, held the mayoral office from 2004 to 2006, and represented Zacatecas in the Chamber of Deputies (the lower house of Mexico's Congress) from 2006 until his passing. They honored a man who subverted politics as usual in local Mexican governance, at one time the exclusive purview of elite landowners, or *hacendados*. Once the little guy himself, Bermúdez always presented his life story as a perennial underdog story – replete with all-black *Norteño* outfits or the *costumbre* of the Mexican *vaquero* in his Stetson cowboy hat, and Tony Lama boots. Yet, the sensationalistic accounts of the Tomato King as the quintessential immigrant success story often masks the nightmare it has become for Latino immigrants in this day and age to try to secure their piece of the American Dream.[12]

The Dream turned Nightmare on the flipside: the unsolved 2007 murder of Santiago Rafael Cruz highlights the underbelly of a deeply flawed immigration system. Cruz, at the time of his murder, was working as an organizer for the Toledo-based farmworkers' union, the Farm Labor Organizing Committee (FLOC). FLOC's most successful labor campaigns have been in the engineering of third party contracts whereby workers, growers, and firms (such as Campbell's Soup, Vlasic Pickles, and the Mount Olive Pickle Company) enter into voluntary agreements that recognize collective bargaining rights with FLOC representing workers. Most recently, FLOC has successfully fought to represent H-2A temporary visa migrant farmworkers in negotiating terms of employment with the North Carolina Growers' Association. Cruz had been on the job for less than a month where he helped to maintain seniority and recruitment lists for potential H-2A workers seeking employment in the tobacco, cucumber, and other crops in North Carolina. His brutal murder in Monterrey, Mexico exposed a corrupt system of labor recruitment that nets *coyotes* thousands of dollars per migrant seeking safe passage to the United States. It is a multi-million-dollar business for *enganchadores*, or labor contractors, who create the migrant streams connecting local communities in Mexico with US destinations where their labor is so heavily in demand (from meatpacking towns, urban gateways, suburban destinations, high-amenity resort towns, to agricultural destinations). FLOC had unwittingly stumbled upon a long-known story of crooked *coyotes*, a system of bribes, exorbitant fees, corrupt government officials, and police forces and border patrol looking the other way, with the overall result of marginalizing an entire class of undocumented migrants who were looking for gainful employment in the worst-paid sectors of the US economy.

The life stories of both Santiago Rafael Cruz and Andrés Bermúdez are important windows into what immigration scholars refer to as transnationalism, or "making parts of one's life simultaneously in more than one country" (Smith 2006: 210). In this chapter, we explore the various features of transnationalism that currently define the strong connections between Latin America and the United States. We discuss earlier sociological approaches to the issue of immigrant incorporation and how Latino immigrants force the sociological conversation beyond the assimilation/cultural pluralism impasse:

> Constructing transnational political spaces should be treated as the resultant of separate, sometimes parallel, sometimes competing projects at all levels of the global system – from the "global governance" agenda of international organizations and multinational corporations to the most local "survival strategies," by which transnational migrant networks are socially constructed. (Guarnizo and Smith 1998: 6)

In defining transnationalism as a third way, we are following the lead of Guarnizo and Smith in differentiating between transnationalism from above (mostly covered in the next chapter on globalization) and transnationalism from below. The specific iterations of local survival strategies (often referred to as transnational social fields or grassroots forms of transnational lives) include the experiences, remittance economies, hometown associations (HTAs), and dual citizenship. The role of the state is present in each of these sections so we will highlight its role in shaping transnational lived experiences. Finally, we discuss the limits of transnationalism in the resurgent US nationalist response to immigration. We pay particular attention to the rise of militarizing the border, mass deportations and sweeps, vigilante groups, and punitive anti-immigrant ordinances stemming from Hazleton, Pennsylvania to the state of Arizona. We analyze this backlash in reference to the prevalence of neoliberal nativism and the racialization of Latino immigrants.

The Melting Pot: Creamy Soup or Chunky Stew

Most are familiar with the melting pot myth – that the United States, as a nation of immigrants, is defined by the melting of immigrants into "American" culture.[13] Many assume that the melting pot is both a normative ideal and an empirical inevitability. The assimilation and cultural pluralist positions both view American culture as a melting pot. In the first position, the melting pot produces a homogeneous product much like a creamy soup. In other words, the differences are smoothed out to guarantee that each spoonful will taste the same. American culture is thus defined as a homogeneous product and thus all Americans are essentially the same. The assimilation position often posits that all immigrants will conform to the established (white, Anglo-Saxon, Protestant) or the "American middle class" ways of living. A cultural pluralist position would characterize the melting pot as the container of a chunky stew. Differences are allowed to coexist in the same pot because the different tastes tend to complement one another in the formation of one big stew. This is often described as life in the hyphen as American culture represents an amalgamation of ethnic traits defined as Irish-American, German-American, Mexican-American, etc. The two melting pot metaphors – regardless of whether they contain a homogeneous identity that immigrants must assimilate into *à la* the creamy soup analogy, or posit that American identity is an amalgamation of different national identities coming together to form a unity in diversity *à la* the chunky stew analogy[14] – are quite specific to the turn-of-the-twentieth-century European immigrant experience. Today's Latino immigrants experience their incorporation into US culture much differently (as a direct result of racialization, neoliberal nativism, and transnationalism).

Since the origins of the discipline of sociology in the United States, a major preoccupation with the US approach to immigrant incorporation has been front and center (see Omi and Winant 1994: 14–23; Hirschmann 1983; Portes and Rumbaut 2006; Park and Burgess 1921: 734–84; Alba and Nee 2005; Bulmer 1984). In fact, the origins of US sociology arose concomitantly with massive demographic changes in the US population. Due to the large influx of Southern and Eastern European immigrants into the urban centers of the East Coast and Midwest, the US population was losing its white, Anglo-Saxon, Protestant numerical dominance. To account for these changes, scholars in the nation's first Sociology Department at the University of Chicago started with the basic query of US turn-of-the-century society: how does "American culture" absorb the shifting immigrant stock without significantly altering what it means to "be an American?"[15]

The focus on migrant adaptation and what immigrants had to do to acculturate prefigured the possible range of explanations to either one of assimilation (immigrants viewed as the uprooted) or cultural pluralism (old world traits transplanted). Unfortunately, the focus on how immigrants were received by the host society became increasingly a non-question (John Higham's [2002] seminal history on nativism, *Strangers in the Land*, points to this oversight). Any urban problems were treated as a question of cultural maladaptations in the same way that discussions of the so-called "Negro" problem also looked for the source of problems in Blacks, not how Blacks were treated by Whites. Rather than studying the insidious effects of nativism and racism, the Chicago School was content to view social problems as one of cultural maladjustment.

American sociology developed the notions of assimilation and cultural pluralism to signify the range of cultural adaptations by

Southern and Eastern European immigrants. It was the work of Thomas and Znaniecki (1918–20) that further refined migration studies by focusing on the "conditions of departure" and "conditions of arrival" for Polish migrants to the United States. Their use of the life history method exposed them to a variety of sources on the lives of Poles in both Poland and the United States. The five volumes of *The Polish Peasant* consist of personal letters and diaries, court dockets, newspaper reports, autobiographies published in immigrant newspapers, and a small number of oral accounts.

The degree to which migration induces social disorganization is one of the key points of Thomas and Znaniecki's analysis. "[M]ost of the motives which actuated the peasant in the old country either do not exist any longer or are greatly weakened [in the United States], precisely because all social ties are loosened" (Thomas and Znaniecki 1984 [1918–20]: 281). But preventing the immigrant from reverting to what the authors refer to as "complete wildness" was "the social spirit of the immigrant, to his tendency to form groups, to his traditional ability for social organization" (289).

Old world traits of the Polish immigrants would serve as the sources to draw upon for constructing a "genuine Americanization." For Thomas and Znaniecki, the shift from traditional to modern society was synonymous with assimilating the European peasant to the "American" way of life. Embedded in their analysis is an explicit modernization thesis of turning backward peasants, through the use of immigrant-built institutions, into genuine Americans prepared for the fast-paced, ever-changing life of modernity. The change required taking peasants who assumedly led sheltered village lives, experienced unchanging social circumstances, depended solely on oral communication with like members of their group, remained completely passive in the larger matters of the day, and molding them into cosmopolitan, Americanized citizens.

During the same time-period, a Mexican anthropologist named Manuel Gamio was collecting the life stories of 76 Mexican immigrants and four US-born Mexican Americans. The studies culminated in the publication of *Mexican Immigration to the United States* and *The Mexican Immigrant: His Life Story*. The research was funded by the Social Science Research Council and the resultant publications were first released in 1930 and 1931, respectively. Gamio was an anthropology student of Franz Boas, who was the first anthropologist in the United States to develop notions of culture similar to the Chicago School tradition, so the personal interviews Gamio collected addressed topics – migration and settlement patterns, social and cultural adaptation, and inter- and intra-ethnic interactions – that were very similar to the issues of concern for Thomas and Znaniecki (see Gutiérrez 1995: 61; Sánchez 1993: 120–3). Gamio would eventually become sub-secretary of public education (1924–5) in post-revolution Mexico and would dubiously promote the ideology of *indigenismo* to root Mexico's national culture in its pre-Columbian origins.

As opposed to the inevitable assimilation that characterized the Chicago School studies on European migration, Gamio focused on how immigrants from Mexico retained their Mexican identities in the face of a particularly oppressive set of conditions and many immigrants' subsequent disdain for anything equated with becoming "American." As respondent Don Antonio from Leon, Guanajuato told Gamio in 1926, "I don't have anything against the *pochos*, but the truth is that although they are Mexicans, for they are of our own blood because their parents were Mexicans, they pretend that they are Americans. They only want to talk in English and they speak Spanish very poorly. That is why I don't like them" (Gamio 1931: 58).

The disdain by this respondent for those Mexicans – *pochos* – who try to "act American" runs counter to the assimilationist view that immigrants will become increasingly Americanized over time and will eventually conform to the dominant group's expectations. Yet, Gamio is rarely cited in discussions of cultural pluralism because Mexican immigrants have been largely ignored by historians and sociologists interested in migration for the majority of the twentieth century.[16] The "cultural pluralism" of Mexican immigrants and other Latinos is much more complicated than existing cultural analyses of European migrant adaptation precisely because of the factors of racial exclusion, which have not figured prominently in the sociological study of migration.

Transnationalism as a "Third Way"

Out of this melting pot impasse, sociologists at the end of the twentieth century began to question the very terms of the debate that assumed immigrant incorporation was only relevant to the receiving nation. Beginning with research on Dominican immigrants to New York City and Boston, scholars such as Grasmuck and Pessar (1991) and Levitt (2001, 2004) began to identify that events in the lives of Dominican immigrants were not divorced from events in the communities they, often temporarily, left behind. Thus began the conversation on transnationalism as both lived experience and an analytical frame for immigration studies.

In Levitt's (2001) *Transnational Villagers*, she looks at the linkages between the Dominican community in Boston that is concentrated in the Jamaica Plain neighborhood. She finds that the majority of immigrants come from the same small community near Baní named Miraflores. Rather than following the prescribed course of cutting ties with the homeland and easily melting into the US mainstream, Levitt notes that Dominican immigrants are reinventing both homelands as one interconnected community in the areas of religious practices, electoral politics, community development, and gender and family relations. She introduces the concept of social remittances to account for "the ideas, behaviors, identities, and social capital that flow from host- to sending-country communities" (Levitt 2001: 54).

Today, what it means to be Dominican is lived out as much in the upper west side Manhattan neighborhood of Washington Heights as it is in Santo Domingo, as New York City is now the second largest Dominican city (larger than Santiago, which sends the majority of migrants to Washington Heights). To be Ecuadorian or Colombian is lived out expressly in Corona, Queens as much as it is Bogotá or Quito. At the translocal level, Rouse (1991) identifies that what it means to be Aguillan from Michoacán is expressed just as strongly in Redwood City, California. Linkages abound between Aguacatán, Huehuetenango, Guatemala and Morganton, North Carolina (Fink 2003); Ticuani, Puebla and New York City (Smith 2006); and Miraflores, Dominican Republic and Jamaica Plain, Boston, Massachusetts (Levitt 2001). These interconnected communities are all important expressions of how: "Today, immigrants develop networks, activities, patterns of living, and ideologies that span their home and the host society" (Basch et al. 1994: 4).[17] We believe the important thing to draw from the sociological debate on labels and linguistic qualifiers is that "trans-migrants" (those who actually move back and forth between nations) are not synonymous with transnationalism (a social process of interconnected communities through the flow of people, information, capital, commodities, and identities) and thus those practices, actions, social networks, and flows of information are best understood at the community level (Levitt 2001: 13–15; Smith 2006: 12). We are not convinced that these transnational connections are new phenomena as there are longstanding examples of binational linkages within Mexican and Puerto Rican sending and receiving communities. The circular migration of transmigrants has linked villages in Zacatecas and Fresno for well over 70 years, and the longstanding back-and-forth movement of Puerto Ricans between San Juan and El Barrio, Bronx, New York City also pre-dates the large-scale migration that commenced during the 1940s and 1950s. Given Puerto Rico's commonwealth status that often allows Puerto Ricans to fully express their US citizenship rights on the mainland, a dual affiliation makes sense. The Mexico case points to transnationalism as a much longer historical trend.

Historian David Gutiérrez refers to this longstanding intercon-nection between Mexican American and immigrant communities and sending areas in Mexico as constituting a "thirdspace":

> Having grown used to living, working, and playing in physically separated communities on both sides of the border, members of these transnational social networks often feel as "at home" in one place as another. Of course, on the border, different examples of this transnational sensibility can be seen every day. On the simplest

level, people who live on one side or the other cross the line each day to work, conduct business, or go to school, and for them life in a steadily expanding thirdspace has become routine. At more complex levels, some transmigrants live most of the year in the United States but habitually return to their homes in Mexico to attend village fiestas, tend to business affairs, and participate in baptisms, weddings, funerals, and the many other rites of passage that structure Mexican cultural life. (Gutiérrez 1999: 513)

The core idea of transnationalism is people define their lives simultaneously in more than one nation and it is certainly more easily facilitated in our high-technology-driven information age where families can Skype and IM one another in real time, even if they are living thousands of miles apart.

Latin American governments have sought to recognize and sometimes valorize the role of immigrants by creating official agencies, memorializations, and political representation. In El Salvador, immigrants residing abroad or those affectionately referred to as *"los hermanos lejanos"* are met with a large statue honoring their contributions "on the highway leading from the Comalapa International Airport into San Salvador [that] welcomes returnees to the country" (Rodríguez 2005: 19–20). The Salvadoran state has designated *Departamento 15* as an addition to the 14 states that comprise the nation so that their absence is recognized as constituting the 15th state in the popular and state imaginary. Similarly, the Peruvian state refers to those living abroad as *El Quinto Suyo* or Peru's fifth region. The term is a Quechua derivation that harkens back to Inca spatial logic that identified Peru's Incan Empire (*Tawantinsuyo*) as comprised of four regions. Recognizing migration's central contribution to the Mexican economy, the Mexican state has developed several agencies to represent the interests of those living abroad, from Mexico's External Affairs Department and the more informal services of the Consular to the Program for Mexican Communities Abroad, established in 1991, which has now become the Institute for Mexicans Abroad (*Instituto de los Mexicanos en el Exterior*). The Dominican Republic officially refers to Dominicans Residing in the Exterior and the *Partido de la Liberación Dominicana* (PLD) ran and secured three legislative seats held by candidates residing in the United States, who "officially represent districts on the island but unofficially represent their constituencies abroad" (Levitt 2004: 249). Two other examples include Brazil's Support Program for Brazilians Abroad and Peru's Secretariat of Peruvian Communities Abroad (*Subsecretariado de Comunidades Peruanas en el Exterior*) that was created in 1991 (Berg and Tamagno 2006).

Remittance Economies

The reason why people move is closely linked to the wage disparities and varied employment options among nations. In this era of neoliberalism, it is increasingly difficult to survive in the global south as rich nations get richer and those in the poor nations move. Increasingly, sociologists are referring to remittance economies to explain how the monies generated by immigrants are transferred back to their nations of origin as the main means of economic survival. We will discuss the difference between individual and collective remittances and how Latin American states are recognizing the importance of both forms for economic development.

The reality is remittances constitute one of the most significant sources of income for Latin America and the Caribbean. In 2002, $32 billion were remitted by Latino immigrants. Some $25 billion were remitted from the United States alone so the majority of foreign dollars in the Latin American economy are coming from US Latino immigrants. These are not paltry amounts as they equate to nearly 30 percent of Nicaragua's gross national product and 15 percent of El Salvador's GNP. Table 5.1 provides conservative estimates of the total dollars remitted to select Latin American nations. The amounts include only those dollars officially sent through banks and telegraph services that are registered with both sending and receiving nations.

Better estimates, which include other forms of money transmittal, estimate that $15 billion were remitted to Mexico alone in

Table 5.1. Remittances to Latin America, 2003 and 2006

Latin American Nation	Annual Remittances (2003, US$ millions)	Percent of GDP (2006)	2006 World Bank Estimates (US$ millions)
Mexico	13,266	2.9	24,732
Brazil	5,200	0.4	4,253
Colombia	3,067	2.9	3,929
El Salvador	2,316	18.2	3,330
Dominican Republic	2,217	10.0	3,044
Guatemala	2,106	10.3	3,626
Ecuador	1,656	7.2	2,922
Peru	1,295	2.0	1,837
Cuba	1,194	–	N/A
Honduras	862	25.6	2,367
Nicaragua	788	12.2	656
Bolivia	340	5.5	611
Costa Rica	306	2.3	513
Venezuela	247	0.1	165
Argentina	225	0.3	542
Panama	220	0.9	149

Sources: Inter-American Development Bank, Multilateral Investment Fund (2003); "Migradólares and Remittances" (*Oxford Encyclopedia of Latinos and Latinas in the United States* 2004); World Bank, March 2008, "Migration and Remittances Factbook," http://econ.worldbank.org/WBSITE/EXTERNAL/ EXTDEC/EXTDECPROSPECTS/0,,contentMDK:21352016~pagePK:6416540 1~piPK:64165026~theSitePK:476883~isCURL:Y,00.html.

2003. This constitutes the second largest source of foreign income (after oil and before tourism) and 2006 estimates placed Mexico first in dollars remitted with nearly $25 billion. Other Latin American nations strongly depend on remittances to support their domestic economy. The amount remitted in Honduras constitutes over one-quarter of their gross domestic product. The Dominican Republic, Guatemala, El Salvador, and Nicaragua receive over 10 percent of their GDP via remittances.

Mexico is the exemplar of the recognition that remittances play in local economic development and how they can be used to supplant the evisceration of the public support system (from welfare to infrastructure). During the Vicente Fox administration, the Mexican state adopted their *tres por uno* program, which guaranteed that every dollar remitted via a hometown association (a collective remittance) would be matched by the local, state, and federal governments, or thus a 3 for 1 program. The long-term sending communities in the state of Zacatecas provided the matching example that eventually became the model for the entire nation.

Most often it is at the local level where the impact of remittances is most directly felt. Building clean water systems, sewage systems, new churches and schools, paving roads, providing electrical power, and other basic infrastructure are the main ways that collective remittances are put to use. At the more individual level, remittances within families are designed to provide for those who are least mobile (the elderly, young, and infirm) and least able to provide for themselves economically. Levitt (2004: 244) notes: "In 1994, almost 60 percent of the households in Miraflores [Dominican Republic] said they received at least some of their monthly income from those in the U.S. For nearly 40 percent of those households, remittances constituted between 75 and 100 percent of their income."

Mize interviewed a former *bracero* who sent upwards of 80 percent of his paycheck to cover the costs of constructing his parents' house and paying for his brothers to attend school. "The money was good because we did not have a house [in Mexico]. We sent all our checks and they bought a permit and built a house. I was not married, and my brothers were young, they were studying. So, my money served a purpose, to support them" (interview with Don Jorge de Colima; in Mize 1997).

What remittances provide is really a form of privatizing social reproduction (Burawoy 1976). The costs of maintaining a family are separated by nation-state borders where incomes are generated in the United States but all the subsistence costs reside in Latin America. The flow of remittances, contrary to negative US public opinion, allows US consumers to eat cheap produce, meat, poultry, and seafood while H-2A and undocumented workers are expected to maintain economically viable livelihoods by separating families and communities from wage-earners, or in other words, separating the forces of reproduction from the forces of production.

Hometown Associations

Collective remittances are most often channeled through hometown associations (HTAs) to cover the costs of community development that in earlier eras was the exclusive purview of the state. Funds remitted by immigrants abroad are increasingly building new sewer systems, paving roads, or constructing new public schools in home communities.

Most HTAs, or *clubes de oriundos*, are connected to urban and rural Mexican communities and tend to operate on a small scale for primarily social activities, networks of mutual support, collective yet voluntary remittances, and (on a larger scale) public works projects. "There are eleven statewide umbrella organizations in Los Angeles and Chicago representing the following states: Michoacán, Jalisco, San Luis Potosí, Oaxaca, Zacatecas, Guerrero, Nayarit, Sinaloa, Tlaxcala, Durango, and Guanajuato" (Bada 2005: 311). There are currently over 400 Mexican HTAs in the United States.

When discussing HTAs, it is their novelty that is most often invoked. Yet, scholars of Latino history recognize that longstanding communal organizations have marked the very long history of Mexican and Puerto Rican migration to the United States. Mutual aid societies, the Community Service Organization of the Industrial Areas Foundation (precursors to the United Farm Workers union and Mexican Chicago's Back of the Yards Neighborhood Council), even the settlement house movement popularized by Jane Addams, have marked the long history of Mexican and Puerto Rican incorporation. Yet in their early incarnations, they were almost all aimed at assimilation or Americanizing immigrants. In the case of a few *mutualistas*, the aim was more in terms of maintaining cultural practices or the cultural pluralist incorporation of a Puerto Rican, Mexican American, or Spanish-speaking (Hispano) identity. Sánchez-Korrol's (1994: 131–63) definitive history of Puerto Ricans in New York City identifies the full range of labor union, mutual aid, neighborhood or *colonia*, and special interest organizations that were developed as early as the 1920s in *El Barrio* or Spanish Harlem. Due to the social isolation Mexicans in America endured, many actively formed self-help groups to provide a "broad range of benefits and services [that] they otherwise could not afford" (Gutiérrez 1995: 34).

What makes HTAs unique today is their transnational character. In many ways, the HTAs operate to consolidate many of the other features of transnational living (organizing collective remittances for construction projects, facilitating the enactment of dual citizenship by organizing political constituencies, and providing avenues for information flows that help to shape complex transnational social identities). The transnational mutual aid societies of today are hometown associations that have proliferated among Mexican immigrant communities. Depending on the social networks and migrant flows, US and Mexican local communities are financially interconnected. For instance, "the states of Guerrero, Jalisco, Zacatecas, and Guanajuato account for nearly 70 percent of the membership of all Mexican HTA's in greater Chicago" (Orozco 2002: 88). Additionally, the Mixtec residents of Ticuani, Puebla living in Brooklyn, New York have funded more than two-thirds of the cost of major public works projects in their hometown, exceeding the contributions of federal, state, and local government (Smith 2006: 3).[18] Since 1970, the Puebla community has benefited from migrant remittances by repaving the *zocalo* or public square, installing night lights, constructing schools, refurbishing the church, making potable drinking water, and incorporating the Ticuani Solidarity Committee as a New York recognized nonprofit organization (Smith 2006: 56).

All combined, the states of Jalisco, Michoacán, and Zacatecas accounted for 48 percent of the 3 for 1 projects in 2002 and 64 percent in 2003 (Burgess 2005: 121). Zacatecas alone accounted for the same percentage of projects (36 percent) as all other Mexican states combined (excluding Jalisco and Michoacán). García Zamora's 2004 survey of Jerez, Zacatecas residents found that 60 percent of remittances go to basic living expenses, which leaves very little for infrastructure development projects. Local politics have dramatically shifted to a transnational context where local Mexican electoral races are funded, run, and decided in the United States. HTAs have dramatically shifted the terrain that Mexican immigrants navigate.

Dual Citizenship

With the economic and political support in place for transnational living, a logical extension of seeking a binational social existence is official state recognition of dual citizenship. While HTAs introduced key aspects of civic engagement – funding public works projects, providing vehicles for direct participation in hometown politics, and advocating for the full rights accompanying dual citizenship – due to the preferences embedded in the current US immigration system, the beneficiaries of dual citizenship are more often those from economically and educationally privileged classes. Thus, even though dual citizenship signifies the rights of voting, multiple citizenship identities, and transmigrant practices (easing travel between nations), the rights and privileges are not shared equally by all immigrants.

Within Latin America, there has been a big push in the last two decades to strongly advocate for citizens abroad by allowing dual citizenship. In 1998, Mexico officially designated dual nationality status as an option for Mexicans living abroad and they joined the other Latin American nations that recognize dual US nationality: Brazil, Colombia, Costa Rica, Dominican Republic, Ecuador, El Salvador, Panama, Peru, and Uruguay (Jones-Correa 2001: 998; Galindo et al. 2005: 85). Additionally, Stanley Renshon (2001), writer for the conservative Center for Immigration Studies, notes that Argentina, Belize, Bolivia, Chile, Guatemala, Nicaragua, and Paraguay recognize some form of dual citizenship.

But the recognition of nationality is not the same designation as political citizenship so many of the attempts since nation-state recognition of dual nationals is to push for the full attendant rights of dual citizenship (something the United States is still reluctant to fully allow). At the beginning of this chapter, we discussed the political forces that allowed the Tomato King, Andrés Bermúdez, to hold political office. The struggle for recognition of foreign nationals in Mexican elections is really a struggle over full attendant rights of dual citizenship. Yet Mexico is following the lead of nations such as Colombia, which is the first nation to elect a representative for dual nationals in their lower house of congress: "a special electoral jurisdiction for non-resident nationals and reserving a seat in the lower house for their representation" (Escobar 2004: 48). There are longstanding debates about whether dual citizenship facilitates inclusion in both nations or favors the sending nation more than the receiving. But what is clear is that dual citizenship is clearly prominent and will likely become more prominent as transnational citizens organize their lives simultaneously in more than one nation.

The Limits on Transnationalism: Racialization and Neoliberal Nativism

In his prescient analysis of California's Proposition 187, the so-called "Save our State" initiative, anthropologist Leo Chavez discusses the attempt by California voters, approved in 1994, to deny access to public benefits for undocumented immigrants residing in the state. It began a groundswell of anti-immigrant rhetoric in the mid-1990s that we contend has taken on a renewed momentum in the twenty-first century. Chavez's (1997: 73) chapter notes "the current wave of immigration reform proposals reflect a nationalist response to this transnational challenge." It was written before Proposition 187 was dismissed by state courts and subsequently superseded by two federal acts in 1996 (the Welfare Reform Act or officially the Personal Responsibility and Work Opportunity Reconciliation Act of 1996 and the Illegal Immigrant Reform and Immigrant Responsibility Act [IIRIRA]). Starting with Proposition 187, anti-immigrant forces were clearly defining their battle along racial lines and as a result they took their positions on a range of proposals to overturn the federal Bilingual Education Act of 1974 (Proposition 227-1998), end affirmation action (Proposition 209-1996), make English the official language (Proposition 63-1986), require Latinos to carry identification cards to verify legal residence (connected to the 2010 racial profiling SB 1070 in Arizona), amend the US Constitution to end automatic citizenship for those born on US soil (reintroduced by Nathan Deal [R-GA] as the Birthright Citizenship Act of 2009, HR 1868), trump up fears of a re-conquest or multicultural invasion characterized as threats to national security (a concern only heightened in a post-9/11 US Patriot Act era), and define the contours of the battle over who is or who should be an "American." What Chavez first identified in 1997 is clearly the blueprint for anti-immigrant legislation circa 2010.

Arizona has become ground zero for anti-immigrant sentiments and ensuing legislation. Events in 1997 certainly prefigured the current morass. Decisions made at the national level have created fewer viable border-crossings. Today, Arizona is the main siphon for undocumented immigrants entering the United States. Scholars refer to the situation as the militarization of the border region as heavy surveillance and construction of walls and fences are employed to cut off popular crossing points (Dunn 1996; Andreas 2000; Nevins 2002; Fernandes 2007; Bacon 2008). A series of INS campaigns from 1993 to the present, including Operation Blockade and Operation Hold-the-Line in El Paso, Operation Gatekeeper in San Diego, and Operation Guardian –"Light up the Border" campaign – in Douglas and Nogales, Arizona, have resulted in physically demarcating the line in the sand or the rivers that have symbolically marked the divisions between Mexico and the United States.

In 1993, Border Patrol in El Paso, Texas instituted "Operation Hold-the-Line." With 450 agents in vehicles along the 20-mile stretch of the border to prevent undocumented border-crossings, the enforcement measure attracted national attention. While this operation almost fully eliminated unauthorized crossings, it displaced undocumented border commuters who crossed from Ciudad Juárez on a daily basis to work in El Paso, Texas. Undocumented immigrants who wanted to cross into the United States simply diverted their crossing strategies to more isolated and dangerous parts of the border. In the end, undocumented daily border-crossers were most affected by the implementation of "Operation Hold-the-Line." Importantly, the tactics of this operation were extended to other major crossing points along the border.

With the passage of the IIRIRA in 1996, provision 287g allowed the INS to deputize local police forces as federal immigration officers. Romero and Serag investigated the joint operation between the Border Patrol and Chandler Police Department to target working-class, Chicano neighborhoods in the Phoenix metropolitan area. In what has come to be known as the Chandler Round-Up, the detainment and inspection of papers of those who looked like "illegals," or were of Mexican ancestry, certainly represents racial profiling. It also deployed class profiling, by targeting neighborhoods slated for redevelopment and by stopping pedestrians in public shopping areas, residential streets, unannounced house-to-house visits, and bus stops (Romero and Serag 2005). As cultural critic George Lipsitz (2006) analogizes, if Mississippi defined the 1960s, and California defined the 1990s, it seems that in 2010 Arizona is today's Mississippi – the testing ground of racialized politics.

Things have only worsened since the 1997 Chandler Round-Up. The tactics of stopping anybody who looks illegal, particularly with no probable cause, has become standard police practice under Maricopa County Sheriff Joe Arpaio. McDowell and Wonders (2009/10) interviewed Mexican migrant women and immigrant service providers in Phoenix and Tucson to ascertain the impact of surveillance and racial profiling:

> In every focus group discussion, Maricopa County Sheriff Joe Arpaio emerged as one of the most powerful representations of the complex interplay between surveillance and enforcement rituals as a disciplinary force in the lives of migrants. Although we use Arpaio's name specifically, we are speaking more broadly about what his person has come to embody, not simply the power he holds as an individual. In the lives of many participants, ... he is the "mobile, elastic border," the "gaze of surveillance," and the myriad enforcement rituals that (re)inforce migrants' "illegality" and vulnerability as a disposable source of labor. (McDowell and Wonders 2009/10: 62)

Senate Bill 1070 "Support our Law Enforcement and Safe Neighborhoods" continues the longstanding practice of racial profiling in an increasingly police state. It emboldens law enforcement to verify the citizenship documents of anybody detained who with "reasonable suspicion" may be in the state without proper documents. This bill extends recent legislation in Arizona that followed the lead of California by legislating racist agendas to make English the official language of Arizona (Proposition 106 in 2006), English immersion for limited English proficiency public school students in 2000 (English for the Children – Proposition 203), Arizona's nearly unilateral rejection of the federal recognition for the Dr. Martin Luther King, Jr. national holiday,[19] and rogue racial profiling and intimidation practices by Sheriff Joe Arpaio that hearken back to the vigilante days of the Arizona Rangers. The clear mandate for racial profiling of those deemed "illegal aliens" is in determining reasonable suspicion as it constitutes an explicit penalty for driving while brown or speaking to an officer with an accent. Resistance to the backlash has come from some of the more seemingly unlikely sources: professional sports and popular music.

During the 2010 NBA conference semi-finals, the Phoenix Suns entered the immigration debate by sporting their Los Suns jerseys to celebrate *Cinco de Mayo* with their Latino fans. The jerseys were worn earlier in the season on *Noche Latina* as a marketing attempt to reach their Latino fan base. But Los Suns were also an explicit rejection of the racism aimed at criminalizing all those who "look like" immigrants. The power of standing up to racism is embedded in Los Suns jerseys and explained by Suns managing partner Robert Sarver:

> The frustration with the federal government's failure to deal with the issue of illegal immigration resulted in passage of a flawed state law. . . . However intended, the result of passing this law is that our basic principles of equal rights and protection under the law are being called into question, and Arizona's already struggling economy will suffer even further setbacks at a time when the state can ill-afford them. (cited in Coro 2010)

Fearing an economic boycott, the statement could be read cynically as a corporation taking a stand to protect its economic interests. More interestingly, the roster of the Suns includes three guards from South Africa, Brazil, and Slovenia. Center Robin Lopez is Cuban American and raised in Fresno, California. The team represents a very different composition of Arizona than the one hoped for by the crafters of SB 1070. By making it a state crime for a person to be in the state without immigration documents and empowering the police to interrogate and detain those suspected of being "illegal," the statement by Sarver clearly identifies their rejection of the state law's racist intentions. The designation of Los Suns is also a recognition of the linguistic third-space of Latino immigrants, as technically the team would be *Los Solés* in Spanish but the Span-glish recognition of Los Suns identifies that Latino culture is simultaneously English and Spanish, US and Latin American.

The basketball team was quickly joined by popular music icons in speaking out against SB 1070. Colombian pop singer Shakira was one of the first on the scene to publicly criticize the bill. Her statement at a Phoenix community center expresses a shared sense of *Latinidad* in rejecting the basic tenets of the racial/immigrant profiling law:

> For the past days I have been troubled and continue to struggle internally with law 1070. As a Latina and as someone who believes in equality, I am deeply concerned about the impact Arizona's new immigration law will have on hard-working Latino families. So, I decided to fly to Phoenix yesterday and see the situation first hand. I went to raise awareness about its dangerous consequences and offer my support to the Latino community and to those who defend human rights. . . . If it goes into effect in the next few months, it will not only hurt thousands of hard working Latino families in Arizona, it will also hurt the spirits of the entire Latino community – each of the 45 million Latinos who live and work in the U.S. and who help make this a better nation.
>
> It's understandable that in times of economic crisis fear and confusion take over – people look for someone to blame – but let's not forget what Latinos have given to this country and the workforce that

they signify. Latino immigrants, with and without papers, have generated wealth and economic growth in the United States for generations. It is a misconception that Latino immigrants take away employment opportunities. On the contrary, we help generate them. . . . To the Latino community and all other Americans who oppose this law, please know that I will be with you. Let's keep our spirits up, stay united and protect one another, now more than ever. We've got to join forces and struggle until Congress and the Supreme Court find a just, humanitarian solution to the issue of undocumented immigrants in this country. . . . If there is no problem allowing Latino immigrants to clean our cities, watch over our cars, build our homes, manufacture our products, add to our culture, or drive new business and innovation, then there must be the courage to normalize their situation. I hope America can find that courage, if only for the sake of the human condition: because we are all equal before God and before the law. Let's hope America lives up to the example and message of equality and freedom that this great country has shared with the rest of the world. (Shakira 2010)

Latino Studies scholar María Elena Cepeda (2010: 63) describes Shakira as an idealized transnational citizen. Her music career and "public persona . . . occupies the interstices between the Latin American and the U.S. Latino contained within the rubric of Latinidad." Cepeda goes on to note "her multiple subject positions (as Lebanese-Colombian, Caribbean-Colombian, female, popular performer, and recent U.S. migrant) contribute to a sense of Latinidad and colombianidad both within and outside U.S. borders" (p. 63). With her statements rejecting the tenets and aims of SB 1070, Shakira is also a great example of how a clearly politicized sense of *Latinidad* operates in defense of all Latinos deemed "illegal" in the eyes of the law.

Neoliberal nativism stands at the crossroads where free trade ideology meets up against the criminalization and racialization of Latino immigrants as "illegals" or "illegal aliens." It is a lesson in how the free flow of commodities is eased in the era of the North American Free Trade Agreement (NAFTA) and the Dominican Republic-Central American Free Trade Agreement (DR-CAFTA), while the flow of people is increasingly restricted. The current era of late capitalism increasingly relies upon national and supranational agreements to facilitate capital accumulation by driving down wages, displacing non-capitalist social relations with market and wage labor relations, eviscerating the nation-state in terms of public infrastructure and social services, and creating tariff-free zones to maximize transnational corporate profits. Seemingly, nation-states become more irrelevant as global capital writes the rules of the game in terms of labor relations and environmental safeguards. Yet, as neoliberalism signals the end of nation-state borders, the resurgence in nativist sentiment has created a new Washington Consensus on the issue of border security and the supposed need for further fortification and militarization, in a very thinly veiled adherence to nativism. It is the vigilantes and their media backers that make the violence inherent in militarization manifest in both its logic and practice.

The biggest farce of neoliberalism is that of the laissez-faire state, when in reality the state becomes the preferred labor contractor in the service of global capital. Andreas (2000) argues that boundary enforcement along the US–Mexico border during the 1990s stems from political factors and pressures to gain control of the border. Additionally, he asserts that enforcing the boundaries of the United States is less about curtailing the flow of drugs and undocumented migration than it is about setting the symbolic territorial boundaries of the nation-state as the state has in the past failed to implement immigration policies that would deter the movement of undocumented immigrants along the boundary. As the undocumented are criminalized upon entering the United States, the border has become much more dangerous. With increased enforcement, immigrants have been forced to cross in the least defended stretches of the 2,000-mile border, which are the most treacherous and dangerous crossing points. Sociologists Eschbach et al. (2004) estimate that with the increased border militarization nearly 5,000 immigrants died on the US side of the border from 1985 to 2002.

Lou Dobbs, Glenn Beck, Sean Hannity, and Bill O'Reilly lambast immigrants as unwelcome pariahs on the US economy who are supposedly hell bent on a *reconquista* or takeover of

America, and their words are reproduced in legislation introduced by politicians like Bill Owens (Gov-CO), Rick Santorum (PA), Tom Tancredo (CO), James Sensenbrenner (WI), and Saxby Chambliss (GA). Their foot soldiers are anti-immigrant vigilantes who call themselves Minutemen and vehemently claim their actions are not racist. The presence of citizens' militias and other self-proclaimed defenders of "America" exacerbate the paramilitary and hyper-militarized situation along the US–Mexico border. The American Patrol and Minutemen Project are both self-declared vigilante groups who decided that federal immigration policy is a failure and they will take the law into their own hands to detain suspected undocumented immigrants. The militias have garnered significant media attention but are roughly as effective as a group of paint-ball enthusiasts put in an actual combat situation. Nevertheless, the anti-immigrant rhetoric and actions of the Minutemen have provided a legitimating context for extremely xenophobic legislation such as the Sensenbrenner Bill HR 4437, which would have made it a felony to be undocumented or assist an undocumented immigrant. The bill passed the House by a vote of 239 to 182 but, as mentioned earlier, was not reconciled with a stalled Senate immigration bill before any of its measures were enacted into law. The Minutemen also emboldened Republican representatives to present bills that would have called for mass deportations of "illegals." As a result, some of the largest demonstrations in the history of the nation (the immigrant rights marches of 2006) were organized in most major cities to support immigrant rights, denounce HR 4437, and displace the media spotlight from vigilante approaches to immigration reform.

The symbolic representation of the border as a wall or fence in need of further fortification only serves to place the problems associated with illegal immigration as a burden on those deemed illegal. Lost in the equation are the employers who are illegally employing workers without papers, and politicians on both sides of the aisle who criminalize immigrants for their own political gain. Though the majority of the attention garnered by high-profile sweeps, raids, and deportations identifies the problem as overwhelmingly impacting Mexican immigrants, the recent spate of Dominican deportations in New York City serves to further marginalize the Washington Heights community.

Portugues (2009) identifies that "more than 36,000 Dominicans have been deported since 1996 ... constitut[ing] 25 percent of the incarcerated population in New York State." Since 9/11 and the Patriot Act, it is lawful to indefinitely detain immigrants while their status is being determined. Dow (2004: 9) discusses the rising incarceration of undocumented immigrants. In the early 2000s,

> the immigration agency holds some 23,000 people in detention on a given day and detains about 200,000 annually. The prisoners are held in the INS's [now ICE] service processing centers, in local jails, in facilities owned and operated by private prison companies ... and in the Bureau of Prisons facilities, including federal penitentiaries. Wherever they are held, [ICE] prisoners are "administrative detainees"; they are not serving a sentence.

This has only spread since IIRIRA's 287g provision, which allows local law enforcement to use their prisons for immigration detention, in addition to empowering them to enforce federal law during sweeps, raids, and deportations. "The majority of Dominicans who are deported have committed crimes, often minor ones, including crimes committed many years ago and mostly related to traffic violations or drug consumption." Ryan Shanovic, from the Immigrant Rights Clinic, denounced the continuing deportation process; when deported individuals arrive in the Dominican Republic, they face discrimination. "They face the stigma of being a deported criminal and the only companies that will hire them are American ones" (Portugues 2009).

Conclusion

The idea throughout the chapter is that the analysis and lived experiences of transnationalism require a distinction between transnationalism from above and transnationalism from below. With this distinction, it becomes clearer to understand the varied experiences of diverse Latino immigrants. For example, dual citizenship is easily facilitated for the professional classes migrating from Latin America and thus binational incorporation is relatively easy. What makes the current era so unique for Latino immigrants residing in the United States is the expressions of transnationalism (identity formation, remittances, HTAs, and dual citizenship). Therefore, we posit that the transnationalism from below perspective highlights a third way of conceiving of immigrant incorporation vis-a-vis the dominant assimilation/cultural pluralism debates in sociology. This corresponds with a thirdspace that Latino immigrants increasingly occupy that is neither fully US-based nor fully Latin American-based, but clearly an interstitial mix of both. The nativist and racist challenges to transnationalism ensure that Latinos will never identify fully as part of the US nation.

6

Neoliberalism and Globalization

Álvaro Leonel Ramazzini Imeri, a bishop from San Marcos, Guatemala, has lived most of his life amid civil war, violence, and wanton murder. Born in 1947 in Guatemala City, Ramazzini Imeri was only 13 years old when the civil war began, a war that would continue for the next 36 years. When he recognized his calling to the Roman Catholic Church, Ramazzini Imeri served as a parish priest in San Juan Sacatepéquez, a predominately Mayan community besieged by the violence of the Guatemalan civil war. The village (*pueblo*) endured a reign of despotism as the CIA-backed Guatemalan government-state fought a war of attrition against leftist alliances and indigenous peoples who sought democratic reform, land redistribution, and community self-determination. The war led to the deaths and disappearance (*los desaparecidos*) of over 200,000 people, an estimated 83 percent of whom were of Mayan origin. As the UN peace accords took hold in 1996, Bishop Ramazzini Imeri assisted in authoring the official report of the Guatemalan truth and reconciliation commission (*Comisión para el Esclarecimiento Histórico,* or CEH). In 1998, the Recovery of Historical Memory Project was released, which detailed the human rights abuses associated with the civil war. His co-author, Bishop Juan Gerardi, was bludgeoned to death two days after the release of the report. Ramazzini Imeri feared he would meet the same fate but this was not the first, nor would it be the last, time that he faced violence and death threats.

In addition to his longstanding advocacy for environmental

justice and reducing the impact of climate change, Ramazzini Imeri has worked tirelessly on land reform policies in support of small farmers and landless workers, and human rights. He stated to the Cleveland Catholic Diocese in 2008, "I want all people to understand reality from the perspective of individual dignity so that this dignity will be respected." The Bishop often invokes international human rights, discussed in terms of dignity, justice, and respect, to make his case. As he described to *El Sol de Cleveland*: Bishop Ramazzini explains his motivation:

> the depressed rural world, the worker who with his sweat waters his affliction, cannot wait any longer for full and effective recognition of his dignity, which is not inferior to that of any other social sector. He has the right to be respected and not to be deprived with maneuvers which are sometimes tantamount to real spoliation of the little that he has. He has the right to real help, which is not charity or crumbs of justice, in order that he may have access to the development that his dignity as a person and as a son of God deserves. It is necessary for bold changes, urgent reforms, without waiting any longer.[20]

In a 2004 article advocating for fair trade coffee, he brought to the attention of US Catholic readers that the plummeting coffee prices are resulting in more land concentration in the hands of the wealthy, fewer sustainable methods of growing coffee in the plantation system, and the resultant poverty among coffee pickers. "Bishop Ramazzini ruefully explains that the nation's fourth source of income is 'family in the United States, sending money back, working 18 hours a day to do this'. Even this 'foreign aid' isn't enough to keep many small farmers and seasonal workers afloat these days."[21] The Bishop does not see his church teachings as separate from the current political and economic inequalities in Latin America, but sees his vocation as entrenched in making lives better for those in his congregation and beyond. "The Catholic Church in Guatemala is countering inhuman treatment with active support of workers. In 1992, the San Marcos Diocese assisted the formation of APECAFORMM, a Spanish acronym for The Mam Mayan Association of Small Organic Coffee Producers. They have since allied with *Manos Campesinas*, a sales and export cooperative founded by the neighboring Diocese of Quetzaltenango" (Morrow 2004). The creation of fair trade coffee production, for Bishop Ramazzini Imeri, is fully consistent with his duties and he spends time promoting the network to the United States (primarily through Catholic dioceses), where the majority of coffee is consumed in the world.

This chapter explores the global and economic context in which Bishop Ramazzini Imeri has advocated for greater social rights for Guatemalan indigenous peoples and for those who have migrated to the United States searching for better opportunities. The reality for Latin Americans in general, and in particular, the region's 10 million indigenous peoples, is that free trade policies have increased poverty and threaten the viability of subsistence economies in their respective countries. These conditions transpired in earnest after 1994, with the implementation of the North American Free Trade Agreement (NAFTA), and intensified after 2004 with the passage of the Dominican Republic-Central American Free Trade Agreement (DR-CAFTA). While NAFTA allowed for greater economic integration through international capital investment in Mexico, Canada, and the United States, it actively prevented the diffusion of labor across international borders, which disproportionally affected the poorest of all three trading partners – Mexico – and its people. DR-CAFTA had similarly overlooked provisions for the safe and legal passage of migrants originating in its six free-trading nations: Guatemala, El Salvador, Costa Rica, Honduras, Nicaragua, and the Dominican Republic. The suppression of wages and the opening of traditional Latin American economies to competition from international markets have led to immiseration (or a widening gap between the rich and the poor). Most often these conditions in Latin America propel people to leave their countries searching for jobs and new ways to sustain their communities. Free trade policies have also altered urban and rural demography throughout the Americas by creating global slums in large cities across Latin America and by dramatically altering where immigrants settle and make a living in the United States, often in destinations where previously only few Latino immigrants resided. In so-called new US destinations,

Latino immigrants occupy a range of jobs, including making up a majority of workers in an emergent serving-sector class. Together, the neoliberal policies of NAFTA and DR-CAFTA, which created more productive and integrated economies in the Americas, are responsible for the increase in undocumented immigration from Latin America into the United States.

The Historical Context of Neoliberalism

Latin America has long served as the laboratory for international economic policy, so much of what is shared is a history of colonialism that turned Latin America into a supplier of raw materials to feed, clothe, transport, house, and enrich Europe. As the nascent nations of Latin America and the Caribbean sought to throw off the colonial shackles of Spain, Portugal, Britain, and France, between 1810 and 1824 the majority of Latin American nations became independent nation-states. Yet, the end of colonialism did not result in economic self-determination for most, if not all, Latin American nations. When nations emerged from colonies throughout Latin America, it seemed as though the United States would adhere to the tenets of the Monroe Doctrine (1823) and would guard against the incursion of colonialism from Europe and other parts of the world. Instead US policy makers and robber barons took Latin America for themselves, particularly in the military and economic spheres. Americans racialized Latin Americans as a mongrelized people at best, or as savage Africans and Indians at worst. These racialized images were initially set in motion in the US–Mexico War of 1846–8 that was justified according to the ideology of Manifest Destiny. Arguing that the United States was ordained by God to rule from sea to shining sea, the US quickly filled the power vacuum left by the expulsion of European colonizers as it fought for control of Mexico's northern territories. Mexico was eventually forced to cede nearly one-half of its lands to the United States with the signing of the Treaty of Guadalupe-Hidalgo in 1848. Over the next 50 years, the United States, through official military policy, business tycoons, or filibustering, aimed at controlling more and more of Latin America.

Under the aegis of creating a shipping channel that connected the Atlantic and Pacific oceans, the US government appropriated land from Colombia to build the Panama Canal after attempts by robber barons such as Cornelius Vanderbilt's plans for a Nicaragua Canal fell through. Vanderbilt and his transportation-based empire were emblematic of several US railroad financiers who sought to expand transportation channels and markets into Latin America. Robber barons financed the Mexican railway system, created the shipping lanes, and found other overland routes to expand markets and US business interests. Similarly, the filibusters were motivated by Manifest Destiny, greed, power, and bolstered by official US efforts at controlling the affairs of the Americas writ large. Central to the making of Central America was filibuster, and at one point president of Nicaragua, William Walker. Tennessee native Walker was a staunch supporter of slavery and sought to create a Central American slave-territory first in Baja California and Sonora, Mexico and then in Nicaragua (part of the Federal Republic of Central America). He amassed "colonists" who worked as hired mercenaries to conduct illegal wars until he was overthrown as president of the nation-state he invaded and controlled, Nicaragua. Upon his third attempt to expand the slave empire into Central America, Walker was executed by the Honduran authorities in 1860.

The United States increased its holdings by aiming its sights on the remains of the Spanish Empire during the Spanish–American War. It led to 1898 Treaty of Peace in Paris and subsequent US control of Puerto Rico and the Philippines. The United States did not stop there, however, and without imposing colonial designations, it ruled de facto in much of Latin America (particularly the Spanish Caribbean and Central America). In 1902, the United States passed the Platt Amendment, which subsumed Cuban affairs, both domestic and foreign, under US control. The model of control of Cuban affairs became the model for melding the Monroe Doctrine and Manifest Destiny. Naked self-interest was enough justification for US intrusion into sovereign nations' affairs and this was on full display in the US sponsorship of dictator Rafael Trujillo in the Dominican Republic. The United States occupied the Dominican Republic from 1916 to 1924 and installed each president until 1978. Trujillo, though friendly to US corporate interests, ran the nation as an autocrat for his family's own financial interests. The authoritarian dictator sought to remove Haitian influences over Dominican society, in what was referred to as *el blanqueamiento* or whitening of the Dominican Republic. The campaign eventually led to a border war resulting in the massacre of tens of thousands of Haitians living on the Dominican side (Candelario 2007: 93).

The shared history of Spanish colonialism and US imperialism is certainly what unites Latin America into a shared geopolitical and historical region (see Mignolo 2005; Quijano 2000). Today, it is the forces of neoliberal globalization and particularly the development of free trade agreements that define Latin America's uneven and combined development (Callinicos and Rosenberg 2008; Trotsky 1980 [1932]) in facilitating the conditions for large-scale migration. The contemporary approach to the global economy often exacerbates these inequalities by adhering to a set of principles defined as neoliberalism.

"Neoliberalism is in the first instance a theory of political economic practices that proposes that human well-being can best be advanced by liberating individual entrepreneurial freedoms and skills within an institutional framework characterized by strong private property rights, free markets, and free trade" (Harvey 2005: 2). The neoliberal rhetoric of "freedom" is both a perversion of the term in political theory and an inaccurate representation of the central roles nation-states retain in managing trade and markets. The great facade of neoliberalism is the laissez-faire state, as strong governance is essential for corporate dominance. Increasingly, governance operates in the service of global capital in the arrangement of free trade agreements, and at the supranational levels of the World Bank and International Monetary Fund.

Nearing the end of World War II, the international financial arms were created, according to the US plan for the world economy, during the 1944 Bretton Woods conference. The supranational institutions created at that time were originally the International Monetary Fund (IMF) and World Bank, joined by the World Trade Organization (WTO) and International Finance Corporation (IFC), in 1995 and 1960 respectively. These institutions have set the rules of the financial game in the postwar era and often dictated how nations of the global south pursued economic development by securing loans, aid, and direct foreign investment. Most nations in Latin America, from the worldwide 1930s Depression on, operated on the model of development referred to as import substitution industrialization (ISI). The premise being that national development only occurs when basic industries and manufacturing are built within the nation. The aim is to reduce the dependency on importing the basic commodities for economic development while escaping the earlier dependency that turned the colonies into solely exporters of raw materials.

So, for instance, attempts at national development via ISI strategy were very important to Mexico in the nationalization of their oil industry. By the 1980s, to secure a loan from the World Bank, it was a precondition that national economies would abandon ISI approaches. After the worldwide financial crisis beginning with the oil shock in 1973, the language and accompanying economic policy for securing IMF and World Bank assistance shifted to structural adjustment policies (SAP). Mike Davis (2007), in *Planet of Slums*, writes about the SAP-ing of the Third World by the international divestment in small-scale agriculture and the resultant spatial concentration of poverty in the urban population centers of the global south. SAP policies smack of colonial models of economic development with the condition of creating export-oriented economic activities, requiring privatization and austerity programs, and ending the social safety net. "In return for debt rescheduling, indebted countries were required to implement institutional reforms, such as cuts in welfare expenditures, more flexible labor market laws, and privatization" (Harvey 2005: 29). In 2008, the neoliberal policies of the Washington Consensus were identified as the main source for the financial meltdown that brought the global economy to the brink of worldwide depression.

The United States saw its banking, insurance, financial services, and automobile industries nearly collapse and the US state provided unprecedented monetary support to save corporations "too large to fail."

The ideology of neoliberalism is clearly in crisis (see Bellamy et al. 2009). In Latin America, the last 40 years of debt crises, monetary devaluations, and structural adjustments brought about by SAP development strategies have led to major economic crises and most unexpectedly by those in power, a resurgent socialist response to US imposed economic imperialism. Vehemently opposed to privatization, deregulation, lowering tariffs, and export-oriented production, a clear anti-Washington Consensus is articulated by Venezuela's Hugo Chávez, Bolivia's Evo Morales, and Brazil's Lula da Silva and Argentina's Nestor Kírchner. The last two's signing of the "Buenos Aires Consensus" in 2003 expressly repudiated the policies of the Washington Consensus – a consensus explicitly created to change the terms of Free Trade Area of the Americas (FTAA) negotiations – which eventually broke down talks and has stalled FTAA attempts to this day (Massaldi 2003).

Any and all IMF or World Bank loans secured by national governments are bound to adhere to certain conditionalities such as austerity programs to qualify for debt servicing.[22] As a result, it is often those who are the most vulnerable (those relying upon public safety nets or public goods like education, healthcare, housing, social services, etc.) who pay the costs of SAP and other macroeconomic conditionalities. Over the past ten years, trade liberalization has been the driving force behind US and Bretton Woods institutions' approaches to Latin America. First established by NAFTA among the United States, Canada, and Mexico, the ideology of free trade has dominated the US economic approach to all of the Americas. Followed in 2005 with the agreement that would be ratified as the Dominican Republic-Central American Free Trade Agreement (DR-CAFTA), and the US led hemispheric free trade zone with its lobbying for the FTAA, the goal is to remove tariffs to allow for the free flow of capital and commodities. Never acknowledged is that an accompanying free flow of migrant labor is off the negotiation table during this era of neoliberal nativism (see chapter 5).

These neoliberal reforms in Latin America gear their economies to export and more TNC-led development. As Latin America becomes one of the world's cheap labor sources (both as immigrant laborers and within the region's industrial assembly and production sectors), trade liberalization facilitates yet another attempt at export-oriented development. The agreements establish the preconditions for the growth of *maquiladoras* (or tariff-free assembly plants) along the US–Mexico border, export processing zones in the Dominican Republic, and US corporate access to cheap labor in Puerto Rico's longstanding model of export-based development. For Puerto Rico, this originated during the World War II-era Operation Bootstrap that gave rise to the island's pharmaceutical industry and displaced hundreds of thousands to the United States. Rather than increasing the standard of living as promised by Milton Friedman and the Chicago School proponents of neoliberal globalization, we see a deepening of inequalities that necessitate transnational migration as a survival strategy.

Global Cities and Global Slums

In considering the spatial and organizational aspects of the rising power of TNCs (transnational corporations) and the wealth they generate and concentrate, two sides of same neoliberal coin have led concomitantly to both the development of global cities (Sassen 1998) and the increasing concentration of poverty in the development of global slums (Davis 2007). The massive profits generated by TNCs are concentrated in the business and finance centers of the global economy. Sassen's (1998, 2001, 2005) groundbreaking analysis of the approximately 40 business/finance centers of global economy demonstrates that the long-time centers dominated by London, New York, and Tokyo have been more recently joined by cities in the global south such as São Paulo, Buenos Aires, and Mexico City. "Global cities are centers for the servicing and financing of international trade, investment, and headquarters operations" (Sassen 1998: xxiii). Corporations were able to fully deploy their global reach only after the breakdown of monopoly capitalism that kept corporations bounded by nation-state borders. "Global cities are sites for immense concentrations of economic power and command centers in a global economy" (Sassen 1998: xxv). As TNCs produce goods in the global south by pitting nations against each other in a race to the labor input bottom, they headquarter and concentrate capital in global cities (the disproportionate global north recipients of international migrants), outsource customer service to Asia or Central America, and define the entire globe as potential markets for consumption.

On the flipside, "rapid urban growth in the context of structural adjustment, currency devaluation, and state retrenchment has been an inevitable recipe for the mass production of slums" (Davis 2007: 17). The same processes that concentrate wealth are also concentrating poverty in global slums generated by austerity programs and neoliberal reforms ending welfare, education, public housing, trade protectionism, agricultural subsidies and tariffs. With approximately 1 billion of the world's population residing in a slum, the deep poverty generated under neoliberal regimes pushes nearly 20 percent of the world's population to the sheer brink of existence. Latin American slums in Mexico City, Santo Domingo, Cochabamba, Lima, Quito, Bogotá, São Paulo, Rio de Janeiro, Buenos Aires, and Santiago contain anywhere from 20 percent of each nation's residents (such as Mexico with nearly 20 million slum dwellers) to nearly 70 percent (Peru's percentage of slum dwellers). In Brazil, nearly 37 percent of the nation's population resides in slums or *favelas*, which translates to a nearly inconceivable 52 million dwellers living under conditions of absolute poverty (Davis 2007: 24). It is no surprise that international migration becomes a major option for those seeking to escape poverty.

In discussing the emergent role of the Los Angeles metropolitan area as a global city, Hamilton and Chinchilla (2001: 41) note: "Los Angeles now has the largest Mexican, Central American, Asian, and Middle Eastern populations in the United States, and has the largest populations of Koreans, Filipinos, and Iranians outside of their respective countries." Yet, the flow of Latin American immigrants to the United States is highly variegated. For instance, the recent flow of middle-class and professional immigrants from South America indicates "the large proportion of their number that is foreign-born and their higher socioeconomic standing in relation to other Latino groups" (Espitia 2004: 259). South Americans in the aggregate have higher indicators of socio-economic status than Cubans (the Latino group most often noted for their exceptionalism) but they are highly differentiated within each national origin and subgroup. Jones-Correa (2007: 24) notes that South American Latinos tend to congregate along the global cities of the eastern seaboard (New York City, Washington, DC, and Miami) and are found in much smaller numbers in the US Southwest.

Global migration circuits follow the linkages made at the local community, regional, and national levels. As a result, global cities are disproportionately the recipients of Trade NAFTA (TN) visa holders, H-1B temporary workers, and immigrants who qualify under the employee skills criteria for naturalization. The flow of professional class Latino immigrants is facilitated by a preference for highly educated, skilled labor that defines contemporary US immigration and naturalization law. Those with transnational corporate ties are the least bothered by the processes of border militarization and undocumented (often working-class) immigrant criminalization.

Conversely, a global cottage industry has developed around facilitating the transnational flow of poor people's money. Most are familiar with Western Union, with locations in Wal-Marts worldwide, and usurious check cashing businesses like Money Tree and PayDay, which charge huge interest rates to provide cash advances on payroll checks. These corporations profit off the fact that living without papers means no ability to open bank accounts and too often those living in poverty are not able to get out of the debt cycle caused by losing upwards of 15–30 percent of their weekly paycheck for a cash advance. The chain of the global remittance system connects international banks, wire transfer corporations, governments, foundations, international development agencies, senders, and recipients in virtual flows that criss-cross the globe every second. Smith and Bakker (2008: 93) note the example of Zacatecas hometown associations (HTAs) in Mexico and the statewide network of community development that certainly impacts Zacatecas City and other municipalities within the state and also major migrant communities in Los Angeles and Chicago. Embedded in this network is also Mexico City, where financial resources are both funneled and matched by the federal government. The network includes Denver, Colorado (the corporate headquarters of Western Union), which has made billions in surcharges to transfer money from the United States to Mexico; it includes Brussels, Belgium and Geneva, Switzerland, where international agencies of the United States are increasingly involved in remittance economies. Finally, it includes the institutional support of the Rockefeller Foundation in New York City and the Inter-American Development Bank in Washington, DC. The flow of cash from a migrant to their sending community is integrated in a truly global network flow.

A helpful indicator of inequality is the Gini land concentration index, which provides a measure of the ownership of arable land and how equally or unequally it is distributed (see table 6.1). Partially related to the Spanish colonial land tenure system that placed as much land into the hands of those who were financially capable of holding land in the name of the Spanish crown, the Gini coefficients are the highest (meaning a monopoly land tenure system where the very few own the vast majority of agricultural lands) in Latin America compared to any other region of the world. If one person owned all the agricultural land, the Gini coefficient would be 1.0 and if land tenure was equal where every citizen owned the same amount, the coefficient would be 0.0.

Land tenure inequality clearly defines the western hemisphere, the rates have remained remarkably consistent over time, and the results are a major impetus for migration to cities or abroad. When examining the recent rise in megacities, it is this increasing population concentration that represents the safety valve to increasing land concentration. Table 6.2 identifies the rising megacities in Latin America and how the development policies of

Table 6.1. Land Concentration in the Americas

Nation	Gini Land Concentration Index	Year of Census
Argentina	0.83	1988
Brazil	0.87	2006
Colombia	0.79	1988
Costa Rica	0.81	1981
Ecuador	0.82	1982
El Salvador	0.81	1981
Honduras	0.66	1993
Mexico	0.74	1971
Panama	0.87	1990
Paraguay	0.93	1991
Peru	0.86	1994
Puerto Rico	0.77	1987
United States	0.74	1987

Source: Adapted from http://www.fao.org/economic/ess/world-census-of-agriculture/2000-world-census-of-agriculture/en/.

the last 40 years have resulted in more rural-to-urban migration. Overcrowded cities like Mexico City, São Paulo, Rio de Janeiro, Bogotá, and Lima are witnessing a tremendous rise in *favelas* or *colonias*, temporary housing that is often defined as informal due to the lack of basic amenities like paved roads, sewage systems, and electricity. These deleterious conditions are also factors that result in international migration.

Global Economic Restructuring

The social changes associated with the idea of globalization are bound up with a rise in "free" trade agreements, an ascendant international division of labor, a TNC-led competition of nations providing labor at the cheapest price, and a reordering of production and consumption relations (see Mize and Swords 2010). In the United States, the major changes wrought by globalization are often discussed in terms of the deindustrialization, service economy, new

Table 6.2. Rise of Latin American Megacities
(population in millions)

City	2004	1950
Mexico City, Mexico	22.1	2.9
São Paulo, Brazil	19.9	2.4
Buenos Aires, Argentina	12.6	4.6
Rio de Janeiro, Brazil	11.9	3.0
Lima, Peru	8.2	0.6
Bogotá, Colombia	8.0	0.7

Source: Adapted from Davis 2007: 4.

economy, or post-industrial society. However, the major point of agreement is the United States has irrevocably shifted from its manufacturing-based economy to a service economy and as a result factory towns are better understood as rust belt cities. The urban Midwest and Northeast have most directly suffered the pangs of deindustrialization and many cities are still figuring out survival strategies without a manufacturing base.

Economic restructuring has also had a major impact on the Southwest metropolitan areas. With the massive reduction in manufacturing, the Southwest's base, unlike the Northeast and Midwest rust belt that is still reeling, was quickly subsumed by an ascendant low-wage service sector. In these locales, the vast majority of today's employment opportunities for immigrants consist of work in informal and service sectors. For instance, the restructuring of the Los Angeles economy includes, on the one hand, the decline of traditional, highly unionized, high-wage manufacturing employment and, on the other hand, the growth of employment in high-technology manufacturing, some craft specialties, and the advanced services sectors of the economy. Yet the vast majority of new service sector jobs are contingent, minimum wage, and lacking the economic security that leads to savings, retirement, healthcare, home ownership, and middle-class lifestyles. The reality for many Americans in the service sector is they need at least two jobs to make ends meet and often if they have dependants, their salary still does not bring them above the official poverty line.

For example, South Central Los Angeles – the traditional industrial core of the city – bore the brunt of the decline in heavy manufacturing employment, losing 70,000 high-wage, stable jobs between 1978 and 1982 and another 200,000 between 1982 and 1989 (Johnson et al. 1997: 1073). As the gateway to a middle-class living closed, the loss of steady manufacturing employment contributed to a widening gap between rich and poor. The jobs created in the wake of deindustrialization are, as Waldinger (1996: 1081) notes, minimum wage, no-benefits jobs in the top three industries that employ immigrants in Los Angeles – restaurants, garment producers, and private households.

Beyond Los Angeles, the forces of economic restructuring are shifting employment options to meatpacking plants in the rural Midwest, high-amenity service provision in the Rocky Mountain resort towns, factories and poultry processing in the Southeast, and informal or day-labor jobs in the Northeast. The burgeoning sociological literature on "new destinations" has arisen as a direct result of these large-scale economic changes as it is Latino immigrants who are often filling these low-wage jobs in the janitorial, care work, landscaping, and construction industries. Latino immigrants tend to be concentrated in the carpet factories of Dalton, Georgia; the construction and hotel cleaning industries of ski resorts such as Aspen, Vail, and Park City; Tyson poultry plants throughout the rural Southeast; and the apparel industry in Los Angeles. Day-labor sites, assumed to be a thing of the past, have emerged again in Long Island, Phoenix, Austin, Denver, Queens, Palm Beach, and Langley Park, Maryland to name just a few. The foremost expert is UCLA Professor Abel Valenzuela, who estimates that approximately 100,000 day laborers seek daily work at one of the 400 day-labor hiring sites nationwide, and adds, "I'd say a significant number are Home Depots; not a majority, but a significant number" (Greenhouse 2005). A post-industrial economy has created a plethora of job opportunities in the service sector but the vast majority are low-wage, undesirable work with no benefits or advancement opportunities. Only when addressing why people are increasingly impelled to leave Latin America does the draw of these jobs make sense.

Globalization and Immiseration

Global income and wealth disparities have increased to nearly incomprehensible levels since the rise in neoliberal development policy. Currently more than 1 billion people live on the equivalent of less than US$1 per day. The amount that people are paid for a job is captured by measures of income. In 1980 the median income in the richest 10 percent of countries was 77 times greater than in the poorest 10 percent. By 1999, the gap had grown to 122 times. Yet economic inequality has also increased within many countries. By 1998, close to one-half of the world's population were considered to be living in poverty. Absolute poverty is a UN defined threshold that allows for one standard definition of poverty, in terms of being able to meet the most basic of needs like food, water, shelter, and clothing. In the world, nearly one-quarter live below the absolute poverty line, which indicates the billion on the brink of starvation and not meeting basic survival needs in the face of certain death. Comparing this to the fact that the richest 20 percent controls 85 percent of global wealth, whereas the poorest 20 percent share 1 percent of wealth, it becomes clear how dire circumstances are for the world's poor. Over 8 million people living in Latin America are below the absolute poverty level. A better indication of how widespread poverty is has been the relative poverty line set by each nation to define the income necessary to be able to support one's self and family. In 1998, over 50 percent of Latin Americans lived in relative poverty. Most Latin American nations set their poverty line at US $5–7 per day, which corresponds to the Mexican minimum wage. The amount most low-wage jobs pay Latin Americans in one day can be earned in one hour by Latino immigrants working in the United States.

The gap between rich and poor is stark and on full display in the juxtaposition of the few super-rich billionaires and the billions living in absolute poverty. "More than one billion of the world's population subsist on incomes less than a dollar per day. The richest fifth of the world's population controls 85 percent of the globe's wealth, leaving little more than 1 percent for the poorest fifth. In Mexico, the twenty-four wealthiest families have more money than the twenty-four million poorest Mexicans" (Lipsitz 2001: 9). It seems particularly egregious that in a nation with so much poverty resides the world's richest person. Carlos Slim was identified by Forbes.com as the richest person in the world with a net worth of $53.5 billion in 2010.[23] His wealth was mostly accrued as a result of purchasing Telmex, Mexico's national phone system that was privatized as a result of structural adjustment policies. Today, Telmex has the highest worldwide rate for phone service. Customers pay more to use phones in Mexico than anywhere else in the world. Does Slim care that his fortune is amassed by private monopolization and usurious rates to customers? A recent dinner hosted by Warren Buffett and Bill Gates elicited this response from Slim: "Trillions of dollars have been given to charity in the last 50 years, and they don't solve anything," he said, adding, in apparent reference to the Gates–Buffett "Giving Pledge," "To give 50 percent, 40 percent, that does nothing."[24] In his attempt to corner the Latin American telecommunications market, Slim's spin-off América Móvil has acquired once state-owned, now privatized phone companies in Central America; long distance service in Colombia, Peru, Chile, Argentina, Brazil, and Uruguay; cellular service in Argentina, Uruguay, Brazil, Peru, Ecuador, Puerto Rico, and Colombia; and cable television service in Puerto Rico, Colombia, and Peru. Slim's pattern of wealth generation is clear: leverage buyouts to monopolize national telecommunications and maximize profits by hiking up customer service fees in a non-competitive environment.

Government leaders in Mexico, turning a blind eye to Slim's empire, have long dealt with these massive inequalities by looking northward for economic development opportunities. In 1965, the Mexican government initiated the Border Industrialization Program, which created a free trade border zone that allowed US companies to establish assembly plants, or *maquiladoras*, tariff-free. In 1969, RCA, Motorola, Hughes Aircraft, Litton, General Electric, and other US firms built 72 assembly plants. By 1974, there were 655 US plants and on the eve of NAFTA, in 1992, 2080 plants were in operation, employing half a million workers. The 1994 ratification of NAFTA has resulted in a doubling of the program where in 2005 there were approximately 5000 plants employing 1 million workers who earn between $5 and $10 per day.

From the US perspective, NAFTA was a means of keeping competitive with the European Union trading bloc and Japan's East Asia trading bloc. It was in many ways a last gasp US attempt to recover its lost status as the driver in the global economy. The trade agreement between the United States, Canada, and Mexico loosened trade regulations/tariffs on products imported and exported to each of the nations. It is a very detailed agreement with 24 key provisions that are specific to industries such as textiles, automotive, and agriculture. Even though no single provision addresses the flow of labor migrants, nonetheless NAFTA facilitates the movement of labor (people) due to Mexico's increased emphasis on export agriculture in central and particularly southern Mexico. Subsistence forms of living are displaced when lands are devoted solely to export agriculture, which is why there are proportionally more emigrants leaving Oaxaca, Michoacán, Guerrero, and Puebla. The intent by the US government is to restrict the flow of people northward by fortifying the border and other legislative proposals. Without recognizing that NAFTA has taken away the means of self-sufficiency (access to land for poor rural dwellers) and has driven wages to below subsistence levels, movements have to occur as a survival strategy.

Similar economic conditions in El Salvador and the Dominican Republic are leading governments to pursue the dual strategy of encouraging transnational corporations to set up in export processing zones and fund infrastructure and development projects with remittances from their citizens working abroad. In El Salvador, they are referred to as "*los hermanos lejanos*" and constitute nearly 33 percent of the population. Even though El Salvador endured a civil war to challenge the coffee elite, or 14 families who operated as autocrats, today nearly 90 percent of the nation's wealth is owned by the richest 5 percent. Before the civil war, these 14 families controlled approximately 80 percent of the nation's wealth. The nation has aggressively entered into the call-center business, offering incentives for Dell and GMC to locate their customer services centers in the nation. The US Department of State estimates 300 US corporations doing business in El Salvador, predominately in the production of textiles and apparel, shoes, and processed foods.

In 1998, more than 20 percent of Dominicans lived below the DR official poverty line of only $2 per day. Estimates at the time found that over 50 percent had no running water and over 20 percent lacked electricity. Yet, a period of sustained economic growth during their efforts at trade liberalization resulted in what economists dubbed the Dominican "miracle." Four sectors of the Dominican economy, each with annual growth rates exceeding 10 percent, powered the miracle in telecommunications, construction, tourism, and export processing zone manufacturing. Tourism alone generated more than $4 billion in foreign exchange in 1999. The official measures of growth were impressive, but who profited from the miracle? In the export processing zones, current wages average about $80–120 per month (or $4–6 per day). The 43 zones include more than 400 factories employing 200,000 people and accounted for almost $1billion in exports in 1998. Yet, more than 10 percent of all Dominicans live outside the borders of the Dominican Republic and behind Mexico, the DR is the second largest sender of immigrants to the United States from the western hemisphere. Both the Dominican Republic and El Salvador entered into DR-CAFTA to increase job opportunities in their respective export processing zones. The result is not an increased standard of living for EPZ workers, but more of the same low wages and minimal subsistence living that result in transnational migration circuits for survival.

The New Serving Classes

The hollow promises of privatization, free trade, and export-based development are still touted by adherents to neoliberalism but those who are directly feeling the negative effects of immiseration are not waiting for the profits to trickle down. By filling low-wage jobs with little to no advancement, Latino immigrants are eschewing the formal, yet clearly limited, job opportunities in their home nation and opting more and more for the informal employment options in the United States. A clearly constrained "choice," the reality of limited options for the low-wage workers of the world is often a selection of the lesser of two evils. Sassen refers to the option of working in the United States as a labor migrant as filling the "new serving classes" of the global service economy:

> In addition to employing low-wage workers directly, the expanded service sector also creates low-wage jobs indirectly, through the demand for workers to service the lifestyles and consumption requirements of the growing high-income professional and managerial class. The concentration of these high-income workers in major cities has facilitated rapid residential and commercial gentrification, which in turn has created a need for legions of low-wage service workers – residential building attendants, restaurant workers, preparers of specialty and gourmet foods, dog walkers, errand runners, apartment cleaners, childcare providers, and so on. The fact that many of these jobs are "off the books" has meant the rapid expansion of an informal economy in several major U.S. cities. For a variety of reasons, immigrants are more likely than U.S. citizens to gravitate toward these jobs: these jobs are poorly paid, offer little employment security, generally require few skills and little knowledge of English, and frequently involve undesirable evening and weekend shifts. In addition, the expansion of the informal economy facilitates the entry of undocumented immigrants into these jobs. (Sassen 1998: 48)

To serve the needs of the wealthy or those aspiring to the elitist standards of conspicuous consumption, the serving class jobs of gardeners, general laborers, garment workers, domestics, restaurant workers, farmworkers, hotel maids, janitors, and day laborers are increasingly filled by Latino immigrants. US consumption patterns are relying, at least in terms of maintaining elite consumer demand, on labor-intensive services steeped in neo-bourgeois tastes and sensibilities. "This has reintroduced – to an extent not seen in a very long time – the whole notion of the 'serving classes' in contemporary high-income households. The immigrant woman has replaced the traditional image of the African-American female servant serving the white master" (Sassen 2005: 205).

The new serving classes have arisen with an increase of indigenous immigrants from Mexico and Central America. Often untouched by prior national development projects, indigenous communities in Mexico, Central America, and South America were long able to maintain subsistence ways of living until their land became valued for export agriculture. Further exacerbating their marginalization, corn subsidies to US growers were never struck down by NAFTA and now US corn floods the Mexican market to the point that local, unsubsidized maize farmers cannot compete. Yet the tortilla production monopoly means the price of corn tortillas is at an all-time high so many indigenous communities are being literally starved out of their existence in Oaxaca, Puebla, Chiapas, Veracruz, and Guerrero.

Independent journalist David Bacon has documented the indigenous transnational communities that are picking crops in California, dissembling beef in Nebraska, striking for the right to work in North Carolina, and building coalitions with African Americans in Mississippi.[25] His portraits of stark poverty in the provision of affluence are most striking:

> Triqui migrants from Oaxaca, Mexico work in the fields of prestigious wineries in Alexander Valley and at night return to tent settlements made of plastic-covered bamboo. In Del Mar, one of San Diego's most affluent suburbs, Oaxacan migrants harvest tomatoes, strawberries, oranges, and avocados and, until recently, lived on a hillside within sight of a new housing development. Purepecha farm workers from Michoacan pick lemons in Oxnard, while their families often live in a single room. (Bacon 2010)

The estimates identify a farmworker population that numbers around 744,000 in the late 1990s, with the heaviest concentration of workers employed in the San Joaquin Valley. In the Central Valley, Fresno County is the largest and most profitable agricultural producing county in the world and nearly every conceivable fruit and vegetable is grown in *El Valle*. The Central Coast is host to specialty, yet labor-intensive, crops such as roses and strawberries and nearly 20 percent of the state's farmworkers are employed on the coast.

Los Angeles is the major recipient of Oaxacans but also in large numbers we find indigenous migrants filling important agricultural roles in the Central Valley and along the Central Coast. Among these are speakers of Mixtec, Zapotec, Triqui, Mixe, Chatino, and Amusco, often not fluent in Spanish or English. Assistance for public services is still most often in English and most immigrant service providers in California are geared to assist Spanish-speakers, so the language barrier is important to note. This translational gap is being filled by a variety of indigenous-originated organizations.

In the face of massive displacement and acute poverty, indigenous Mexicans have united in solidarity to protect their communities on both sides of the border. *Frente Indígena de Organizaciones Binacionales*, or the Binational Front of Indigenous Organizations (FIOB) is the largest organization serving indigenous Mexican immigrants residing in the United States. "The *Frente*'s organizing strategy is based on the culture of Oaxacan communities, particularly an institution called the *tequio*. 'This is the concept that we must participate in collective work to support our community', [FIOB coordinator Rufino Domínguez Santos] explains. . . . 'We make efforts so that our communities don't lose their culture, their language, and their traditions'" (Bacon 2002). Civic participation is obligatory in many Mixtec and Zapotec communities so it is possible to receive the request to serve in leadership positions in both Oaxaca and California, regardless of one's current location. In another interview, Domínguez Santos states, "Indigenous people from Oaxaca have been practicing dual citizenship for years, without complications or fear of facing the true problem. Many of us return to govern our hometowns as the townspeople mandate, and we continue to help out with the *tequio*, and this gives us the right to be called citizens of the place where we were born, where we work, and where all our dead are buried" (in Martínez-Saldaña 2004 : 130–1).

In the face of globalization, indigenous communities redefine themselves in a transnational context and sometimes expressions of indigenous identity are more likely to be expressed in the United States than in their home communities. Festivals such as the

Guelaguetza (a Zapotec word referring to reciprocity but which has become an ethnic festival) in San Diego, Fresno, and Los Angeles are rivaling the model in Oaxaca City. Another example is a pre-Columbian Mixteco ball game now played in California more than in Oaxaca. While the lack of public space has reduced the game to be played on the one remaining court in Oaxaca City, the game is played in: "a parking lot in Los Angeles' Griffith Park, a lot adjacent to a farm in Selma, a high school sports field in the agroindustrial city of Watsonville" (Fox and Rivera-Salgado 2004: 19). This Oaxacalifornia transnational experience began with the plummeting of coffee prices and dwindling state sub-sidies due to neoliberal reforms, and was exacerbated with the NAFTA-induced corn crisis among Mexican producers, making it increasingly difficult to reside in rural indigenous regions.

Mayans from Guatemala find themselves similarly situated, so from Los Angeles to Providence, Rhode Island, from Immokalee, Florida to Morganton, North Carolina, transnational indige-nous communities are forming where employment opportunities abound. In upstate New York, it is the dairy industry that brings Guatemalans to the area. Fink (2003) offers a rare glimpse into how migrant streams begin. "'I called a good friend of mine in a Mississippi poultry operation', said [human resources manager] Beecher, 'and asked him what he was doing to get people. And he put me on to the Guatemalans'. From his employer-friend Beecher learned of a Catholic church in West Palm Beach, Florida, that was helping Guatemalan refugees working in the citrus belt around Indiantown, Florida" (Fink 2003: 17). Beecher visited during the citrus season's downtime and successfully recruited the first Mayan immigrants to the Case poultry plant in Morganton, North Carolina. Foxen (2007: xvi) notes that the Quiché Mayans who moved to Providence "were working in the jewelry and textile factories and fishing industries that formed an important part of the region's economy."

The struggle for respect and dignity is carried on by Guatemalan-born activist Juan García. Employed as a community organizer with Saint Teresa's Catholic Church, he set up the *Comité de Inmigrantes en Acción*, Immigrants in Action, to secure amnesty for the undocumented population. The efforts of the *Comité* have been slowed due to the overall nativist reaction to the bombing of the World Trade Center. Yet, using models of self-education reminiscent of Brazilian author Paulo Freire, the pre-9/11 work of García was helping undocumented workers educate themselves about their rights and mobilize for amnesty. Since that time, he has coordinated his efforts with local Middle Eastern activists in challenging racial profiling. He has also worked with immigrant workers/labor organizers who lost their fish-processing jobs after organizing and detailing abuses and careless workplace practices that led to the death of one undocumented worker. The need for amnesty becomes all the clearer within this context. García's *Comité* is part of a nationwide network of amnesty advocates that organized the Immigrant Workers Freedom Ride of 2003 and participated in the 2006 immigrant rights marches.

Conclusion

The unique status of indigenous migrants has serious ramifications for international human rights law. The human rights of refugees, migrants, minorities, and indigenous peoples are one area where the United Nations has been able to extend protections and impel national governments to ensure fair and equitable treatment. In many ways, the international human rights regime began with the 1948 Universal Declaration of Human Rights. Hernández-Truyol (2008: 790) offers a helpful approach to human rights in terms of "three 'generations' of rights: (1) civil and political rights (first generation), (2) social, cultural, and economic rights (second generation), and (3) solidarity rights (third generation)." Indigenous communities also have the right to self-determination, autonomy, and sovereignty so the question becomes how are these rights extended to groups embodying transnational lives. The three most pertinent articles from the first defense of human rights are particularly germane for those opposing the forces that are dislocating indigenous communities and impelling migration:

Article 13. (1) Everyone has the right to freedom of movement and residence within the borders of each state. (2) Everyone has the right to leave any country, including his own, and to return to his country.

Article 14. (1) Everyone has the right to seek and to enjoy in other countries asylum from persecution. (2) This right may not be invoked in the case of prosecutions genuinely arising from non-political crimes or from acts contrary to the purposes and principles of the United Nations.

Article 15. (1) Everyone has the right to a nationality. (2) No one shall be arbitrarily deprived of his nationality nor denied the right to change his nationality.

The UN Declaration on the Rights of Indigenous Peoples, adopted in 2007, adapts the human rights declaration but assumes most often that indigenous communities or nations are settled, and so questions arise in the transnational context. Pertinent articles include:

Article 3. Indigenous peoples have the right of self-determination. By virtue of that right they freely determine their political status and freely pursue their economic, social and cultural development.

Article 10. Indigenous peoples shall not be forcibly removed from their lands or territories. No relocation shall take place without the free, prior and informed consent of the indigenous peoples concerned and after agreement on just and fair compensation and, where possible, with the option of return.

Article 20. Indigenous peoples have the right to maintain and develop their political, economic and social systems or institutions, to be secure in the enjoyment of their own means of subsistence and development, and to engage freely in all their traditional and other economic activities.

In considering the massive dislocation of indigenous peoples from southern Mexico, Guatemala, and increasingly South America, what rights do they secure when they leave their homelands for economic survival? Is the doctrine of neoliberalism and economic forces wrought by globalization consistent with the international human rights regime? These questions will become all the more salient as more indigenous communities become permanent residents in the United States.

7

Conclusion: Fronteras Nuevas/ *New Frontiers*

In the rural Oaxacan region of San Juan Mixtepec, indigenous communities are increasingly turning to paid farm work as their means of survival. Filemon López is a community organizer who has worked in the fields most of his life but similar to his compatriots, his employment options are not to be found in his home region in southern Mexico. López's youth was spent working in the fields that brought him to, among other locales, Madera, California. Similar to fellow Mixtecs cultivating tomatoes in Homestead, Florida or picking tobacco in North Carolina, López followed the California migrant trail that is increasingly populated by indigenous migrants from southern Mexico. "The U.S. food system has long been dependent on the influx of an ever-changing, newly-arrived group of workers that set the wages and working conditions at the entry level in the farm labor market. The indigenous workers are already dominant in many of the most arduous farm labor tasks (e.g. picking raisin grapes and strawberries)" (Mines et al. 2010: 2).

Strawberry production is a particularly labor-intensive activity as the delicate nature of the fruit necessitates a great deal of manual, arduous work. Hours stooped over in the direct sunlight coupled with it being the lowest paid sector of the US economy is a ready recipe for attracting the most desperate and marginalized of laborers. Today, that translates to indigenous Mexicans who travel to the United States, often without work authorization papers, to toil in today's factories in the fields. Since the 1990s, the situation has only worsened for those most often neglected by both the US and Mexican governments since the implementation of the North American Free Trade Agreement.

Since the passage of NAFTA and DR-CAFTA, the main corporations associated with strawberry production (primarily Driscoll's and Dole) have shifted more of their operations onto transnational levels. Now, Driscoll's operates berry farms in central Mexico (three in Jalisco and one in Michoacán). Independent growers in Jocotepec, Los Reyes, Tapalpa, and Zamora are exclusively contracted to provide berries during the off-season when North American operations in California, Baja California, New Jersey, Florida, Oregon, Washington, and North Carolina are not able to grow the sensitive fruit. Recent contracts in Chile and Argentina ensure that strawberries are available to US consumers year round.

The community of Jocotepec is particularly interesting in this respect, in that this recent Driscoll's outpost is comprised of transnational migrants (both émigrés and Mexican migrant laborers) who can track activities in their hometown and correspond about all matters via sites such as jocotepec.com and other blogs. The residents themselves meanwhile are often in the United States providing the needed labor inputs for US agribusiness as employment options are more plentiful and better paid than the Driscoll's operation that established organic operations in the municipality in 2009.

Dole owns and controls every aspect of its fruit production processes. With a longstanding presence in Latin America, the vertically integrated Dole Corporation has fed the US consumer utilizing Latin American land and labor since its days as the Standard Fruit Company setting up the banana republic in Honduras and overthrowing the monarchy in Hawaii under the company efforts of Castle and Cook and the Hawaiian Pineapple Company. Today,

Dole produces bananas directly from owned plantations in Costa Rica, Ecuador and Honduras as well as through associated producers or independent growing arrangements in those countries and others, including Guatemala and Colombia. Dole owns approximately

33,600 acres in Costa Rica, 3,900 acres in Ecuador and 28,400 acres in Honduras, all related to banana production. Dole owns approximately 8,100 acres of land in Honduras, 7,300 acres of land in Costa Rica and 3,000 acres of land in Ecuador, all related to pineapple production. The company also owns a juice concentrate plant in Honduras for pineapple and citrus. Pineapple is grown primarily for the fresh produce market. Dole grows grapes, stone fruit, kiwi and pears on approximately 1,900 acres owned or leased by the company in Chile. The company owns or operates 11 packing and cold storage facilities in Chile. In addition, the company operates a fresh-cut salad plant and a small local fruit distribution company in Chile. Dole owns and operates a packing and cooling plant and a local fruit distribution company in Argentina.[26]

The larger presence in Latin America is not resulting in more plentiful job opportunities that keep residents rooted in local communities. Rather, the rewriting of land law (particularly in Mexico as part of the requirements for NAFTA) translates into less land available for subsistence farmers and Latin American governments' inability to protect crops against cheap subsidized competition by US firms. Prices are on the rise for local staples in southern Mexico but their own locally grown crops cannot compete with imports from the United States. For example, in Mexico the price of corn tortillas has increased 279 percent (Henriques and Patel 2004). Since tortilla prices were subsidized until 1996, manufacturers have transferred increased costs to consumers. Additionally, two monopoly firms, GIMSA and MINSA, account for 70 percent and 27 percent respectively of the tortilla market (Henriques and Patel 2004).

Back in Madera, home to one of the largest Mixtec populations in the United States, the crops and agribusiness firms that draw immigrant workers to the area have long shaped the migrant stream into California's Central Valley. What has changed is the ever-increasing scale of production with the monopoly firms that dominate not only the area but have increasingly expanded their reach to global markets and production sites. Also changing is where the workers are coming from to tend the world's fruit and vegetable basket. "The concentration of Mixtec workers has grown so large . . . that a local school recently hired a bilingual aide to help communicate with migrant children and their parents. . . . The bilingual aide speaks only Mixtec and Spanish. He is taking English lessons" (Mydans 1995).

The current state of sociological analyses of Latino immigration provides helpful markers of what we know about social identities, *Latinidad*, pathways to citizenship, cultural citizenship, gender, labor, acculturation, transnationalism, neoliberalism, and globalization. Yet, there are so many unanswered questions and unexplored areas of inquiry as a direct result of Latino communities being ignored or rendered invisible. If the immigrant rights movement was about undocumented immigrants coming out of the shadows of the law, the current sociological focus on new Latino destinations, transnationalism, and neoliberal nativism is similarly about bringing latent issues to the surface for all to see and understand. In this concluding chapter, we want to highlight emerging issues (predictions, topics, and trends) that will certainly influence the lived experiences of Latino immigrants and all Americans for years to come.

The results of the 2000 US Census proclaimed a major demographic transformation that surprised most scholars who track population dynamics. For the first time, Latinos were identified as the largest minority group in the United States. CBS News reported the story as: "Hispanics have surpassed blacks as the nation's largest minority group." The growth of the Latino population, predominately due to relatively higher rates of immigration, as of 2010 stands at 16.3 percent of the overall US population (50,477,594 Latinos in a nation of nearly 309 million residents). In terms of predictions, we have discussed the impending majority–minority population trends and particularly the role of Latinos in becoming both the largest minority group and being on pace to become the largest group, outright, or the majority, by century's end. What are the implications for the non-white majority and how will US politics and identity change as a result? As much as this question pertains to Latinos, it is really a question for the United States and the Americas more broadly if the initial attempts at neoliberal globalization and post-national citizenship are any indications of a future set of hemispheric relations without borders. Of course this question is bracketed by the patterns of resurgent nativism we are witnessing today.

Latino immigration has surfaced as a central political source of balkanization as the majority of the public discourse characterizes immigration as a problem. It is conceived of almost exclusively in terms of Mexican clandestine migration to the United States. What seems clear is that the unsustainable do-nothing rapprochement between the political parties will only last for so long. It is true, if regrettable, that both US political parties have committed themselves to increased border security and the criminalization strategy (e.g., the Obama administration touts it is deporting more undocumented residents at record rates, more than the Bush administration). Yet, there is tremendous dissension within both parties on what to do with the estimated 11 million undocumented immigrants currently residing within the United States. A range of proposals from new Bracero or temporary worker programs, legalization or amnesty protocols, mass deportations, workplace raids, no-match lists resulting in fired employees, high-tech identification requirements, and further criminalization comprise the current range of deliberations on comprehensive immigration reform. The overall trend is to view Latino immigration as a problem, a question of border security, and a source of unwelcome competition with native workers and taxpayers.

If the ideals of the United States hitherto are compared to African American experiences (from slavery to the Civil War, from Jim Crow to the Civil Rights revolution), then the United States in the twenty-first century will likely need to address how Latino experiences will be defined as a civil rights issue, an immigration problem, or something completely distinct. The potential Latino majority is most often mentioned in terms part demographic fact, part anti-Latino hyperbole, part emancipatory hopes and dreams, and part continuation of a long history of marginalization and exploitation. In many ways, Latino immigrants represent the future of the United States itself. How Latinos respond to anti-immigrant sentiments, how they steer the course long traversed by earlier immigrant groups of incorporation and maintaining linkages with nations of origin, and how the US white racial majority reacts to its impending minority status are clearly the defining open questions of the twenty-first century and Latinos are at the center of the maelstrom.

We have sought in this book to illuminate the drivers in this demographic revolution, to shed light on a deeply misunderstood and often vilified community by examining the following: the use and understanding of the term "Hispanic"; cultural, class, and linguistic diversity among Latino immigrant communities; *Latinidad* as a category of inclusion and pan-Latino identity irrespective of citizenship status; the impact of new labor struggles in an era of globalization; and emerging themes of Latino immigration in the United States.

Clearly, Latinos are not a monolithic, homogeneous group. As much as we have discussed the heterogeneity of experiences and identities among different national origins groups, it is really the tip of the iceberg when considering the differences within the national origins. This is central to studying Latinos as the question becomes: do we compare national origin based identities in terms of how the United States racializes Latinos by homogenizing their Hispanic-ness, or, do we compare internal markers of difference along *indio-mestizo* lines, Afro-Latinos, "white" Latinos, and specific subgroups like Chinese Mexicans, Japanese Peruvians, and Sephardic Jewish Cubanos? Is it possible to study both internal and external forces at the same time?

This question of identity begs a conversation about the role of coalitions in both politics and identity formation. We discussed briefly in the previous chapter the attempts at Latino–Middle Eastern–Arab coalition building and the expressed solidarities in opposition to the Patriot Act extension of indefinite detainment and racial profiling. Does the immigrant rights movement signal the beginning of an immigrant solidarity movement across all national origins? Coalitions with the African American community are neither natural nor forced but how do contingent alliances become anti-racist movements? The media crave "Black–Brown" tensions, but is the wedge hype or reality?

Too often, all Latinos are defined as immigrants and as much as we have guarded against this stereotype, we have nonetheless given short shrift to the importance of multiple generations of Latinos who are not themselves immigrants, who may or may not speak Spanish, and may or may not identify with their immigrant neighbors. The Southwest is home to fifth- and sixth- generation Mexicans who are at times living alongside recent immigrants from Mexico and Central America. It appears that in places like Los Angeles, new immigrants are replenishing Mexican culture, and multiple generations currently celebrate, for example, the very recently introduced cultural festival of *Guelaguetza*, so that Oaxacalifornia is experienced by multiple generations of Mexican Americans. Importantly, Latinos in Milwaukee, Detroit, Minneapolis, Chicago, and the Pacific Northwest are also multiple generations and the question becomes how are the 2+ generations treating new arrivals? Are their struggles viewed as shared or bases for competition?

The processes of racialization extend beyond how Latinos are racialized or how definitions of race in Latin America differ from US race definitions. An increasingly self-defined group, identifying as multiracial Latinos, are becoming more noticeable in the United States through the significant rates of Latino intermarriage with all non-Latino groups. Will intermarriage become more prominent and what will that do for a nation that for so long has defined race as an either/or option? This question is increasingly forced by popular culture icons who frequently identify their biracial ancestry. From Shakira to Selma Hayek and Frida Kahlo, are these public figures our bridges to a sustained conversation about multiraciality?

The popular media are so important here, due to their prominence in introducing and framing the world beyond the confines of one's neighborhood and immediate experience. The questions that arise from the entire spectrum of media representations of Latinos have been the source of several books. Even though most Americans may pass over the Spanish-language television stations when flipping channels, the rise of Univision, Telemundo, Galavision, Televisa, and TV Azteca (to name but a few) draws millions of viewers into a shared sense of Latino identity. Increasingly, US channels such as CNN, Fox News, Discovery, ESPN, and other channels are offering Spanish-language equivalents.

The role of language in the future of the United States points to both the rarity that the United States clings to as one of the last normatively monolingual nations and to the 34.2 million Spanish-speakers and nearly 20 percent of the US population that speak a language other than English in the home. The rest of the nation is catching on to what marketing executives already recognize: Spanish-speakers are a long-term force that will not be willed or ignored away and they are increasingly the major source of profits for the most successful Univision. *Telenovelas*, or soap operas, are one genre that typifies Latin American television. These evening shows are part drama, part romance, but one of the most watched genres in the world and currently making Univision the fourth or fifth most watched network in the United States (only barely behind ABC, CBS, NBC, Fox, and in direct competition with the CW).

US representations of Latinos and Latinas are still grappling with the long history of discriminatory and typecast portrayals. The most prevalent media stereotypes of Latino men are as inherently violent (*West Side Story*, *Scarface*, and the Mexican bandit in the Western genre) and of Latina women as hyper-sexualized spitfires (from images of pop singers like J Lo and Shakira to Sofía Vergara's Gloria character on ABC's *Modern Family* and Selma Hayek's pre-Frida movies). As of late, these stereotypes were combined and deftly subverted in the hyper-sexualized, hyper-violent anti-heroines of *Machete* (played by Jessica Alba and Michelle Rodriguez). Director Robert Rodriguez approaches movie making like a graphic novel and his over-the-top portrayals of violence and stereotypes are intended as mockery. Yet, a longstanding stereotype of the Mexican spitfire began with a movie of the same name, as played by Lupe Vélez (1940).

A hangover from the spitfire stereotype is the longstanding obsession in the media with the physical appearance of Latina stars. Shakira accentuates the focus with her song "Hips Don't Lie" and Christina Aguilera directly challenges the preoccupation with her song "Beautiful." The nonstop coverage of Jennifer Lopez's backside and Shakira's hips are clear signals of the objectification of Latina bodies. As a result, low self-esteem and eating disorders tend to be highly correlated with Latina girls who express concern about their body image. Images of beauty for Latinas in the United States and women in Latin America are strikingly similar in terms of skin tone so a whole variety of beauty products are available to remove arm hair, lighten skin tone, change brown eye color with contacts, straighten hair, and lighten hair color. The media images bombard young girls who are the targets of these products. The damage done goes well beyond Latina girls' key market demographic years.

Health trends for Latino immigrants point to several unanswered questions and contradictory outcomes. One finds that obesity, diabetes, and other preventable diseases highly associated with poverty are concentrated among Latinos. The Centers for Disease Control and Prevention has identified significant racial disparities in healthcare and health outcomes. The ten most frequent causes of death for Latinos (in 2006) were: (1) heart disease, (2) cancer, (3) unintentional injuries, (4) stroke, (5) diabetes, (6) chronic liver disease and cirrhosis, (7) homicide, (8) chronic lower respiratory disease, (9) influenza and pneumonia, and (10) certain conditions originating in the perinatal period (Centers for Disease Control and Prevention 2009: table 28). Several causes are related to lack of preventative care, obesity, and poor dietary habits. Yet, when examined by major health outcomes, Latinos often outlive their non-Latino cohorts. Latinos tend to have comparatively low rates of infant mortality. Public health researchers refer to these outcomes as the Latino epidemiological paradox as the high rates of poverty and lack of access to healthcare should predict the exact opposite outcomes. Explanations from migrant self-selection, alternative healer access known as *curanderas* and *parteras* (midwives), diet, to region of country have been hypothesized but many questions still remain. Rumbaut (1997: 932) consistently finds in his research that assimilation is bad for Latinos' health: "For example, low-birth weight (LBR) rates were significantly higher for (more acculturated) second generation U.S.-born women of Mexican descent compared with (less acculturated) first generation Mexico-born women, despite the fact that the latter had lower socioeconomic status, a higher percentage of mothers over 35 years of age, and less adequate prenatal care."

Finally, the work of David Hayes-Bautista et al. (2002) links the baby boom cohort with new Latino immigrants to identify a trend that will only become more pronounced over the next decade. He identifies that a relatively young Latino cohort are mostly of working age and will be the largest growing group of workers whose payment into social security will support the baby boom retirement generation (what he refers to as the simultaneous Browning and Graying of America).

The last issue that impacts not only Latinos but every human on earth is the impending environmental crisis related to global climate change. Latino communities are accustomed to dealing with environmental hazards as too often immigrant and minority neighborhoods are the targets of environmental racism. Peña (1998, 2005) argues that a Chicano ecological consciousness is taking root in Chicano politics as the longstanding recognition of land, sustainable agriculture, and water wars have corollaries with urban struggles over hazardous waste sites, clean air, and industrial pollution. The challenges that lie ahead in dealing with the current ecological threats have a social movement component (in terms of how Latino organizations interface with grassroots mobilizations such as the World Social Forum, faith-based communities, and even corporate solutions like green technology adoption). The future of Latinos is in so many ways wrapped up with the future of the United States, the Americas, and the world.

Notes

1 http://www.image-archeology.com/olvera_street_los_angeles.htm.
2 For a thorough breakdown of hate crimes by ethnicity and national origin bias, see table 1, "Incidents, Offenses, Victims, and Known Offenders" (FBI 2009).
3 The 1990 Latino population in Suffolk and Nassau counties was 165,238. Rate of increase is calculated by dividing the numerical increase by the original population size. All data are from the US Census (*1990 and 2000 Summary Tape File 1* and *American Community Survey 2006–2008 Three-Year Estimates*) and accessed on American FactFinder (http://www. factfinder.census.gov). See also the Pew Hispanic Center's report on the demographic profile of Hispanics in New York: http://pewhispanic.org/ states/?stateid=NY. Accessed April 21, 2011.
4 Not from nowhere, but from a nationwide network of immigrant amnesty advocates who first organized the Immigrant Workers Freedom Ride of 2003. The National Coalition for Dignity and Amnesty is comprised of labor unions, church organizations, civil rights organizations, immigrant rights organizations, community-based organizations, and elected officials. Together, they coordinated the Freedom Rides connecting the struggles of undocumented immigrants with the struggle against racial segregation of blacks in the southern United States during the Civil Rights movement. The most prominent labor unions (SEIU, UNITE-HERE, FLOC, UFW, and UFCW) who have been working to organize the undocumented sponsored, along with original Freedom Ride organizers and national immigrant advocacy organizations, rode on buses in their cross-country journey to Queens, New York for a rally in support of a blanket amnesty program. The Freedom Riders were successful in publicizing the plight of the undocumented in local newspapers but the hoped-for huge media event with strong national television coverage did not materialize.
5 Statistics as they relate to migration rates or protest participation rates are

notoriously unreliable. Estimates utilized to arrive at the 5 million participants in the immigrant rights marches are dependent mostly upon the accuracy of the Los Angeles marches as they constitute approximately 60 percent of all participants. Bada, Fox, Zazueta, and García utilize media accounts to estimate between 3 and 5 million participants but they did not include counts of rallies in some meatpacking and college towns so we are confident in citing their upper limit, as our independent assessment of a smaller sample of marches (but including the largest in Los Angeles, Chicago, Phoenix, Denver, and Dallas) corroborates the 5 million rate (Bada et al. "Immigrant Rights Marches, Spring 2006." http://www.wilsoncenter.org/topics/docs/Database%20Immigrant%20Rights%20Marches.pdf. Accessed May 1, 2011.

6 *Braceros*, as temporary workers, were not counted in the Census rolls and their numbers are not accounted for in the Spanish population estimates of that time.

7 Aired originally on October 7, 2010 but can be found online at: http://www.billoreilly.com/show?action=latestTVShow.

8 The case of deporting Dominicans was covered in http://www.csmonitor.com/2006/0217/p06s02-woam.html and Salvadorans in http://www.latimes.com/news/local/la-me-gang30oct30,0,6717943.story.

9 *Tamales* are one example of traditional Mexican cuisine, pre-dating Spanish contact, which involves the process of wrapping corn husks (*ojas*) around corn meal (*masa harina*) with assorted chile meat and dessert fillings.

10 With the exception of the Tejana society for single and married women, *mutualistas* tended to be male-dominated and usually class-stratified in their organization. In Laredo, Texas, four women-only *mutualistas* were formed separately from the city's nine male mutual aid societies but all too often, women were assigned to gender-stereotyped roles and served in ladies auxiliaries to the males-only *mutualistas* (Orozco 1995: 13). Notwithstanding the gendered aspects, progressive efforts of *mutualistas* included *La Orden Hijos do América* that was organized around "the right to serve on juries, the right to sue an Anglo, and the right to use the public beaches along the coast of Corpus Cristi" (Hernández 1983: 73).

11 The agricultural ladder refers to an old concept (mostly myth) in agricultural economics that upward mobility in the farming industry begins as a field hand, progresses to a crew boss, small farm owner, large farm owner, and finally agribusiness management. The reality is like most social mobility studies, the most likely predictor of one's socioeconomic status is parents' socioeconomic status, and mobility is quite rare.

12 Source materials for the detailing of Bermúdez's life story include Mexico and US newspaper reports (*Los Angeles Times*, *Reforma*, *El Sol de Zacatecas*, *La Jornada*, and *Imagen*), scholarly interviews (Quinones 2008; Smith and Bakker 2008; Bakker and Smith 2003; Smith 2006), and *Municipio de Jerez*

websites that detail Bermúdez's transnational life. The scant media coverage and complete lack of scholarly analysis of Cruz's life story was bolstered by FLOC website coverage.

13 We hesitantly use the term American as we fully recognize that the term represents two continents and it is certainly a misnomer when it is conflated with only the United States. After all, it is the Americas; but we retain the term here to demonstrate that assimilation is often a thinly veiled proscriptive imputation of Americanization.

14 Introducing new metaphors for cultural pluralist approaches tends to confuse the deep affinities with assimilation approaches. We thus avoid the saiad bowl (very popular on standardized tests in secondary social studies exams and self-published books such as Eva Kolb's *The Evolution of New York City's Multiculturalism: Melting Pot or Salad Bowl* [2009, Books on Demand], but not deeply developed as a scholarly concept), kaleidoscope (Fuchs 1990), and mosaic (Gibbon 1938) metaphors for cultural pluralism or multiculturalism (see Taylor 1994). The other metaphors are steeped in horticultural analogies between the uprooted (Handlin 1951) and the transplanted (Bodnar 1985). But we contend that both assimilation and cultural pluralism agree on the United States as melting pot metaphor, the source of contention is what constitutes the contents of the pot. Transnationalism, in many of its forms, is really a questioning of pots, roots, and other nationalist holdovers from the mass movement of Europeans to the United States at the turn of the last century.

15 The Chicago School's preoccupation with the "race problem" at the turn of the century set the terms of debate on how to view immigrant cultures, racial groups, and adjustment in a host society. As the theoretical concepts were initially formed in works such as Park and Burgess' *Introduction to the Science of Society* (1921), Park and Miller's *Old World Traits Transplanted* (Park and Miller 1921), and E. Franklin Frazier's *The Negro Family in the United States* (1939), they were heavily influenced by the dominant philosophical trends at the time. These studies were problematic in that they partially relied upon evolutionary thinking (particularly as a result of the dominant trends of Social Darwinism in turn-of-the-century US sociology), were dependent on "Americanization" as the model for assimilation, and contained views of race that substituted cultural maladaptation for the then-reigning notion of race based on biological inferiorities (Bulmer 1984). In addition, a lack of a concrete economic analysis, in the early research conducted by the American sociologists, implied the conclusion that both racial minority and immigrant *cultures* were the source of backward or peasant-like ways that were particularly maladaptive to the modern metropoles of turn-of-the-century US society.

16 Most sociologists of immigration and ethnicity have uncritically accepted the bifurcation between "old" and "new" immigrants to the United States.

The definitive statements on ethnicity by Alba and Nee (2005) and Gans (1979) employ the assimilation concept to all immigrant groups based on the old/new immigrant distinction. Steinberg (1989) applies the notion of assimilation strictly to "white ethnics." The assumption behind this split is that only Europeans migrated to the United States from 1607 to 1965 (Archdeacon 1983). According to most immigration scholars, the passage of the Immigration and Nationality Act of 1965 resulted in the influx of "third world" migrants (i.e., anywhere other than Europe) that constitute the "new" immigrants to the United States (Reimers 1992). The history of the United States as strictly a European destination before 1965 and strictly an Asian and Latin American destination post-1965 is more wishful thinking than historical reality (see McWilliams 1990 [1948]; Takaki 1993 for decisive counter-evidence).

17 In the sociological literature on transnationalism, it is extremely important to note that the term is highly contested and each author who discusses transnationalism does so in their own unique way and often with their own modified language. We have no intention of providing definitive and mutually exclusive definitions of transnational life, transnationalization, transnationalism (from above and below), transmigrant, transborder, trans-locality, transnational social fields, and the (trans)-nation. Rather, we seek to clarify that many of these terms are deployed to capture transnationalism as either a newly emerging social process or a new framework for analyzing longstanding relations of immigrants in their sending and receiving contexts. Transnational social fields (Basch et al. 1994: 7, 267–8, Itzigsohn et al. 1999; Levitt 2001), transmigrants (Portes et al. 2002; Guarnizo et al. 2003), translocal or translocalities (Smith and Bakker 2008), transnational life or transnationalization (Smith 2006), transborder (Stephen 2007), and (trans)-nation (Cepeda 2010) are different iterations of attempting to analyze sets of social relations that are clearly heightened in this information age that facilitates the easy flow of communication, money, commodities, political power, people, and social networks across nation-state borders. We retain the term "transnationalism" to discuss grassroots deployments of these information, economic, political, and social networks from below.

18 "Ticuani" is a pseudonym.

19 "[A]ll three Arizona House Republicans including current Senator and former presidential candidate John McCain, voted against the bill in '83. The state did not vote in favor of recognizing the holiday until 1992, not only rejecting pleas from Reagan and then Arizona governor Evan Mecham but also losing the NFL's support when the league moved Super Bowl XXVII from Sun Devil Stadium, in Tempe, to California in protest. Arizona was not the only state openly contemptuous of federal law." *Time Magazine*, "A Brief History of Martin Luther King Day." http://www.time.com/time/nation/article/0,8599,1872501,00.html#ixzz0qluNByN3.

20 Cleveland Catholic Diocese. 2008. "Bishop Alvaro Ramazzini Imeri of Guatemala to Speak and Hold Workshop in Cleveland." *El Sol de Cleveland* online, August 22. http://www.elsoldecleveland.com/news.php?nid=858&pag=1&st=0.

21 http://www.americancatholic.org/messenger/feb2004/feature1.asp. Accessed May 12, 2011.

22 http://www.imf.org/external/np/exr/facts/conditio.htm.

23 http://www.forbes.com/2010/03/09/worlds-richest-people-slim-gates-buffett-billionaires-2010-intro.html. Accessed October 10, 2010.

24 Email communication from National Institute for Latino Policy (September 30, 2010). On file with authors.

25 http://dbacon.igc.org.

26 http://www.dole.com/servedocument.aspx?fp=documents/dole/DoleFacilities_LatinAmerica.pdf. Accessed April 20, 2011.

References

Acuña, Rodolfo. 1988. *Occupied America: A History of Chicano*, 3rd edition. New York: Harper and Row.

Acuña, Rodolfo. 1996. *Anything but Mexican: Chicanos in Contemporary Los Angeles*. New York: Verso.

Acuña, Rodolfo. 2010. *Occupied America: A History of Chicanos*, 7th edition. Upper Saddle River, NJ: Prentice Hall.

Alba, Richard and Victor Nee. 2005. *Remaking the American Mainstream: Assimilation and Contemporary Immigration*. Cambridge, MA: Harvard University Press.

Anderson, Benedict. 2006. *Imagined Communities*, new edition. New York: Verso.

Andreas, Peter. 2000. *Border Games: Policing the U.S.–Mexico Divide*. Ithaca, NY: Cornell University Press.

Archdeacon, Thomas J. 1983. *Becoming American: An Ethnic History*. New York: Free Press.

Armstrong, Robert and Janet Shenk. 1982. *El Salvador: The Face of the Revolution*. Boston: South End Press.

Arredondo, Gabriela F. 2008. *Mexican Chicago: Race, Identity and Nation, 1916–39*. Champaign: University of Illinois Press.

Bacon, David. 2002. "Grassroots: Cross-Border Organizing." *Z Magazine Online*. http://www.zcommunications.org/cross-border-organizing-by-david-bacon. Accessed January 31, 2007.

Bacon, David. 2008. *Illegal People: How Globalization Creates Migration and Criminalizes Immigrants*. Boston: Beacon Press.

Bacon, David. 2010. "Living Under the Trees." http://dbacon.igc.org/IndexPS/news.htm. Accessed October 1, 2011.

Bada, Xóchitl. 2005. "Hometown Associations." Pp. 310–12 in *The Oxford Encyclopedia of Latinas and Latinos in the United States*, edited by Suzanne Oboler and Deena Gonzalez. New York: Oxford University Press.

References

Bakker, Matt and Michael Peter Smith. 2003. "*El Rey del Tomate*: Migrant Political Transnationalism and Democratization in Mexico." *Migraciones Internacionales* 2: 59–83.

Balderrama, Francisco and Raymond Rodríguez. 2006. *The Great Betrayal: Mexican Repatriation in the 1930s*, revised edition. Albuquerque: University of New Mexico Press.

Banks, Andy. 1991. "The Power and Promise of Community Unionism." *Labor Research Review* 10(2): 17–32.

Basch, Linda, Nina Glick Schiller and Cristina Szanton Blanc. 1994. *Nations Unbound: Transnational Projects, Postcolonial Predicaments and Deterritorialized Nation-States*. New York: Routledge.

Bellamy Foster, John and Fred Magdoff. 2009. *The Great Financial Crisis: Causes and Consequences*. New York: Monthly Review Press.

Benhabib, Seyla and Judith Resnik (Eds). 2009. *Migrations and Mobilities: Citizenship, Borders and Gender*. New York: New York University Press.

Bennett, Claudette. 2000. "Racial Categories Used in the Decennial Censuses, 1790 to the Present." *Government Information Quarterly* 17(2): 161–80.

Berg, Ulla Dalum and Carla Tamagno. 2006. "*El Quinto Suyo* from Above and from Below: State Agency and Transnational Political Practices among Peruvian Migrants in the US and Europe." *Latino Studies* 4(3): 258–82.

Bishop, Katherine. 1990. "U.S. Adopts New Policy for Hearings on Political Asylum for Some Aliens." *The New York Times*, December 20. http://www.nytimes.com/1990/12/20/us/us-adopts-new-policy-for-hearings-on-political-asylum-for-some-aliens.html?ref=katherinebishop. Accessed July 7, 2011.

Bodnar, John E. 1985. *The Transplanted: A History of Immigrants in Urban America*. Bloomington: Indiana University Press.

Brown, Joye. 2008. "Teens Made Sport of Assaulting Hispanics." Long Island Immigration Alliance, November 21. http://www.longislandimmigrantalliance.com/.../news-_Teens_made_sport_of_assaulting_Hispanics.pdf. Accessed April 20, 2010.

Buckley, Cara. 2008. "Teenagers' 'Violent Sport' Led to Killing on Long Island, Officials Say." *The New York Times*, November 20.

Bulmer, Martin. 1984. *Chicago School of Sociology: Institutionalization, Diversity and the Rise of Sociological Research*. Chicago: University of Chicago Press.

Burawoy, Michael. 1976. "The Functions and Reproduction of Migrant Labor: Comparative Material from Southern Africa and the United States." *American Journal of Sociology* 82(5): 1050–87.

Burgess, Katrina. 2005. "Migrant Philanthropy and Local Governance." Pp. 99–124 in *New Patterns for Mexico: Observations on Remittances, Philanthropic Giving, and Equitable Development*, edited by Barbara J. Merz. Cambridge, MA: Harvard University Press.

Callinicos, Alex and Justin Rosenberg. 2008. "Uneven and Combined

References

Development: The Social-relational Substratum of 'the International'? An Exchange of Letters." *Cambridge Review of International Affairs* 21: 77–112.

Camacho, Alicia Schmidt. 2008. *Migrant Imaginaries: Latino Cultural Politics in the U.S.–Mexico Borderlands*. New York: New York University Press.

Candelario, Ginetta E.B. 2007. *Black Behind the Ears: Dominican Racial Identity from Museums to Beauty Shops*. Durham, NC: Duke University Press.

CBS New York. 2010. "6th Teen Sentenced in Patchogue Hate Crime Death." September 1.

Centers for Disease Control and Prevention. 2009. http://www.cdc.gov/nchs/data/hus/hus09.pdf#028. Accessed April 20, 2011.

Cepeda, María Elena. 2010. *Musical ImagiNation: U.S.-Colombian Identity and the Latin Music Boom*. New York: New York University Press.

Chavez, Leo. 1997. "National Responses to the Transnationalist Challenge." In *Immigrants Out!*, edited by Juan Perea. New York: New York University Press.

Chavez, Leo. 2008. *The Latino Threat: Constructing Immigrants, Citizens, and the Nation*. Stanford, CA: Stanford University Press.

Chmiel, Mark. 2001. *Elie Wiesel and the Politics of Moral Leadership*. Philadelphia: Temple University Press.

Coro, Paul. 2010. "Phoenix to Wear 'Los Suns' Jerseys for Game 2 vs. Spurs: Suns Owner Robert Sarver Issues Statement on New Arizona Immigration Law." *The Arizona Republic*, May 4. http://www.azcentral.com/sports/suns/articles/2010/05/04/20100504phoenix-suns-los-suns-jerseys.html. Accessed July 6, 2011.

Coutin, Susan Bibler. 2003. "Cultural Logics of Belonging and Movement: Transnationalism, Naturalization, and U.S. Immigration Politics." *American Ethnologist* 30(4): 508–26.

Coutin, Susan Bibler. 2007. *Nations of Emigrants: Shifting Boundaries of Citizenship in El Salvador and the United States*. Ithaca, NY: Cornell University Press.

Cranford, Cynthia. 1998. "Gender and Citizenship in the Restructuring of Janitorial Work in Los Angeles." *Gender Issues* 16: 25–51.

Davis, Mike. 2007. *Planet of Slums*. New York: Verso.

De Genova, Nicholas P. 2002. "Migrant 'Illegality' and Deportability in Everyday Life." *Annual Review of Anthropology* 31: 419–47.

De Genova, Nicholas P. 2005. *Working the Boundaries: Race, Space, and "Illegality" in Mexican Chicago*. Durham, NC: Duke University Press.

De Genova, Nicholas P. and Ana Ramos-Zayas. 2003. *Latino Crossings: Mexicans, Puerto Ricans, and the Politics of Race and Citizenship*. New York: Routledge.

Denning, Michael. 1998. *The Cultural Front: The Laboring of American Culture in the Twentieth Century*. New York: Verso Books.

Diaz-McConnell, Eileen. 2003. "Executive Summary." Sabre Systems White

References

Paper *The Hispanic Experience: Analyses over Time and across Data Sources.* http://www.sabresys.com/whitepapers/hispanic_ex.pdf. Accessed May 1, 2005.

Diaz-McConnell, Eileen and Betsy Guzmán. 2003. "Evaluating 2000 Hispanic Data." Sabre Systems White Paper *The Hispanic Experience: Analyses over Time and across Data Sources.* http::www.sabresys.com/whitepapers/hispanic_evaluating.pdf. Accessed May 1, 2005.

Dillin, John. 2006. "How Eisenhower Solved Illegal Border Crossings from Mexico." *Christian Science Monitor*, July 6.

Diskin, Martin and Kenneth Sharpe. 1986. "Impact of US Policy in El Salvador, 1979–85." Policy Papers in International Affairs, University of California.

Dow, Mark. 2004. *American Gulag: Inside U.S. Immigration Prisons.* Berkeley: University of California Press.

Dunn, Timothy J. 1996. *The Militarization of the U.S. Mexico Border.* Austin: University of Texas Press.

Durazo, Maria Elena. 2005. "Making Movement: Communities of Color and New Models of Organizing Labor." *Berkeley La Raza Law Journal* 16: 187–93.

Einaudi, Luigi. 1991. US Ambassador to the Organization of American States (OAS). Prepared statement at a meeting of the OAS Permanent Council Washington, DC delivered on February 14, 1991; US Department of State Dispatch, Vol. 2, No. 8, February 25.

Eschbach, K., J.M. Hagan and N.P. Rodríguez. 2004. "Deaths during Undocumented Migration across the Southwestern Border: What are the Policy Implications in the New Era of Homeland Security?" *In Defense of the Alien* 26: 37–52.

Escobar, Cristina. 2004. "Dual Citizenship and Political Participation: Migrants in the Interplay of United States and Colombian Politics." *Latino Studies* 2(1): 45–69.

Espitia, Marilyn. 2004. "The Other 'Other Hispanics': South American-Origin Latinos in the United States." In *The Columbia History of Latinos in the United States Since 1960*, edited by David Gutiérrez. New York: Columbia University Press.

FBI. 2009. "Uniform Crime Report: Hate Crime Statistics." http://www2.fbi.gov/ucr/hc2009. Accessed April 20, 2011.

Fernandes, Deepa. 2007. *Targeted: Homeland Security and the Business of Immigration.* New York: Seven Stories Press.

Fernandez, Manny. 2010a. "Prosecutors Describe 'Hunt' for Hispanic Victim." *The New York Times*, March 13.

Fernandez, Manny. 2010b. "Teenager Testifies about Attacking Latinos for Sport." *The New York Times*, March 29.

Fernandez, Manny. 2010c. "Guilty Verdict in Killing of Long Island Man." *The New York Times*, April 19.

References

Fernandez, Manny. 2010d. "In Jail, Hate Crime Killer Says He Isn't So Hateful." *The New York Times*, April 29.

Fernandez, Manny. 2010e. "L.I. Man Gets 25-Year Term in Killing of Immigrant." *The New York Times*, May 26.

Ferris, Elizabeth. 1987. *The Central American Refugees*. New York: Praeger.

Fink, Leon. 2003. *The Maya of Morganton: Work and Community in the Nuevo New South*. Chapel Hill: University of North Carolina Press.

Fox, Jonathan and Gaspar Rivera-Salgado. 2004. "Building Civil Society among Indigenous Migrants." Pp. 1–65 in *Indigenous Mexican Migrants in the United States*, edited by Jonathan Fox and Gaspar Rivera-Salgado. La Jolla, CA: Center for US-Mexican Studies, UCSD and Center for Comparative Immigration Studies.

Foxen, Patricia. 2007. *In Search of Providence Transnational Mayan Identities*. Nashville, TN: Vanderbilt University Press.

Frazier, Franklin E. 1939. *The Negro Family in the United States*. Chicago: University of Chicago Press.

Fuchs, Lawrence. 1990. *The American Kaleidoscope: Race, Ethnicity, and the Civic Culture*. Boston: Wesleyan University Press.

Galindo, René, Christina Medina and Xóchitl Chávez 2005. "Dual Sources of Influence on Latino Political Identity: Mexico's Dual Nationality Policy and the Dream Act." *Texas Hispanic Journal of Law and Policy* 11: 74–99.

Gamboa, Suzanne. 2006. "Union Hopes to Build on Houston Success." *Associated Press Online*. http://www.highbeam.com/doc/1P1-117762054. html. Accessed October 1, 2009.

Gamio, Manuel. 1930. *Mexican Immigration to the United States: A Study of Human Migration and Adjustment*. Chicago: University of Chicago Press

Gamio, Manuel. 1931. *The Mexican Immigrant: His Life Story: Autobiographic Documents*. Chicago: University of Chicago Press.

Gans, Herbert. 1979. "Symbolic Ethnicity: The Future of Ethnic Groups and Cultures in America." *Ethnic and Racial Studies* 2: 1–20.

García, María Cristina. 1996. *Havana, USA: Cuban Exiles and Cuban Americans in South Florida, 1959–1996*. Berkeley: University of California Press.

García, María Cristina. 2006. *Seeking Refuge: Central American Migration to Mexico, the United States and Canada*. Berkeley: University of California Press.

García, Mario T. 1989. *Mexican Americans: Leadership, Ideology, and Identity, 1930–1960*. New Haven, CT: Yale University Press.

Gibbon, John Murray. 1938. *Canadian Mosaic: The Making of a Northern Nation*. Toronto: McClelland & Stewart.

Govea, Jessica. 2000. "Mesa Refuge Thursday Presentation." California, September 26.

Grasmuck, Sherri and Patricia Pessar. 1991. *Between Two Islands: Dominican International Migration*. Berkeley: University of California Press.

References

Greenhouse, Steven. 2005. "Day Laborer Battle Runs Outside Home Depot." *The New York Times*, October 12.

Griswold del Castillo, Ricardo and Arnoldo De León. 1996. *North to Aztlan: A History of Mexican Americans in the United States*. Woodbridge, CT: Twayne Publishers.

Guarnizo, Luis and Michael Peter Smith. 1998. "The Locations of Transnationalism," *Comparative Urban and Community Research*, Special Issue: *Transnationalism From Below* 6: 3–34.

Guarnizo, Luis E., Alejandro Portes and William J. Haller. 2003. "Assimilation and Transnationalism: Determinants of Transnational Political Action among Contemporary Immigrants." *American Journal of Sociology* 108(6): 1211–48.

Gutiérrez, David G. 1995. *Walls and Mirrors: Mexican Americans, Mexican Immigrants, and the Politics of Ethnicity*. Berkeley: University of California Press.

Gutiérrez, David G. 1999. "Migration, Emergent Ethnicity, and the 'Third Space': The Shifting Politics of Nationalism in Greater Mexico." *The Journal of American History* 86(2): 481–517.

Habermas, Jürgen. 1998. *The Postnational Constellation: Political Essays*. Cambridge, MA: The MIT Press.

Hamilton, Nora and Norma Chinchilla. 2001. *Seeking Community in a Global City: Guatemalans and Salvadorans in Los Angeles*. Philadelphia: Temple University Press.

Handlin, Oscar. 1951. *The Uprooted: The Epic Story of the Great Migrations that Made the American People*. Boston: Little and Brown.

Harvey, David. 2005. *A Brief History of Neoliberalism*. New York: Oxford University Press.

Hattam, Victoria. 2005. "Ethnicity and the Boundaries of Race." *Daedalus* 134(1): 61–70.

Hayes-Bautista, David E., Paul Hsu, Aide Perez and Cristina Gamboa. 2002. "The 'Browning' of the Graying of America: Diversity in the Elderly Population and Policy Implications." *Generations Journal of the American Society on Aging* 26(3): 15–24.

Henriques, Gisele and Raj Patel. 2004. "NAFTA, Corn, and Mexico's Agricultural Trade Liberalization." *Americas Program*. Silver City, NM: Interhemispheric Resource Center. http://www.cipamericas.org/archives/1009. Accessed July 6, 2011.

Hernández, Jose Amaro. 1983. *Mutual Aid for Survival: The Case of the Mexican American*. New York: Krieger Publications.

Hernández, Kelly Lytle. 2006. "The Crimes and Consequences of Illegal Immigration: A Cross Border Examination of Operation Wetback, 1943–1954." *Western Historical Quarterly* 37(4).

Hernández-Truyol, Berta E. 2008. "Sex, Culture, and Rights: A Re/Conceptualization of Violence for the Twenty-First Century." Pp. 789–92 in

References

Latinos and the Law: Cases and Materials, edited by Richard Delgado, Juan F. Perea and Jean Stefancic. Saint Paul, MN: Thomson-West.

Hesson, Ted. 2010a. "Teens Sentenced in Hate Attack Against Marcelo Lucero." *Long Island Wins* Blog, August 25. http://www.longislandwins.com/index. php/blog/post/teens_sentenced_in_hate_attack_against_marcelo_lucero/. Accessed April 20, 2010.

Hesson, Ted. 2010b. "Nicholas Hausch Sentenced to Five Years in Prison for Attacks on Suffolk Latinos." *Long Island Wins* Blog, October 14. http://www. longislandwins.com/index.php/blog/post/nicholas_hausch_sentenced_to_five_ years_in_prison_for_attacks_on_latinos/. Accessed April 20, 2010.

Higham, John. 2002. *Strangers in the Land: Patterns of American Nativism, 1860–1925*. New Brunswick, NJ: Rutgers University Press.

Hirschmann, Charles. 1983. "America's Melting Pot Reconsidered." *Annual Review of Sociology* 9: 397–423.

Huerta, Dolores. 2008. *A Dolores Huerta Reader*, edited by Mario T. Garcia. Albuquerque: University of New Mexico Press.

Itzigsohn, José, Carlos Dore Cabral, Esther Hernández Medina and Obed Vázquez. 1999. "Mapping Dominican Transnationalism: Narrow and Broad Transnational Practices." *Ethnic and Racial Studies* 22(2): 316–40.

Jabali-Nash, Naima. 2010. "Four New York Teens Sentenced in 2008 Hate Crime." *CBS News*, August 26.

Jenks, Jeremiah and W. Jeff Lauck. 1926. *The Immigration Problem*, 6th revised edition. New York: Funk and Wagnalls.

Jimenez, Maria. 2009. "Humanitarian Crisis: Migrant Deaths at the U.S.– Mexico Border." ACLU of San Diego and Imperial Counties/Mexico's National Commission of Human Rights Joint Report.

Johnson, James, Walter C. Farrell and Chandra Guinn. 1997. "Immigration Reform and the Browning of America: Tensions, Conflicts, and Community Instability." *International Migration Review* 31: 1029–69.

Jones-Correa, Michael. 2001. "Under Two Flags: Dual Nationality in Latin American and its Consequences for Naturalization in the United States." *International Migration Review* 35: 997–1030.

Jones-Correa, Michael. 2007. "Swimming in the Latino Sea: The Other Latinos and Politics." In *The Other Latinos: Central and South Americans in the United States*, edited by José Luis Falconi and José Antonio Mazzotti. Cambridge, MA and London: Harvard University David Rockefeller Center for Latin American Studies.

Joppke, Christian. 2010. *Citizenship and Immigration*. New York and Cambridge: Polity Press.

Kingsolver, Barbara. 1989. *Holding the Line: Women in the Great Arizona Mine Strike of 1983*. Ithaca, NY: Cornell University Press.

Kymlicka, Will. 1996. *Multicultural Citizenship: A Liberal Theory of Minority Rights*. New York: Oxford University Press.

References

Laguerre, Michel. 1998. *Diasporic Citizenship: Haitian Americans in Transnational America*. New York: St. Martin's Press.

Levitt, Peggy. 2001. *Transnational Villagers*. Berkeley: University of California Press.

Levitt, Peggy. 2004. "Transnational Ties and Incorporation: The Cases of Dominicans in the United States." Pp. 229–56 in *The Columbia History of Latinos in the United States Since 1960*, edited by David Gutiérrez. New York: Columbia University Press.

Lewthwaite, Stephanie. 2009. *Race, Place, and Reform in Mexican Los Angeles: A Transnational Perspective, 1890–1940*. Tucson: University of Arizona Press.

Lipsitz, George. 2001. *American Studies in a Moment of Danger*. Minneapolis: University of Minnesota Press.

Lipsitz, George. 2006. *The Possessive Investment in Whiteness: How White People Profit from Identity Politics*, 2nd edition. Philadelphia: Temple University Press.

Little, Michael R. 1994. *A War of Information: The Conflict Between Public and Private U.S. Foreign Policy on El Salvador, 1979–1992*. Lanham, MD: University Press of America.

Lorence, James J. 1999. *The Suppression of Salt of the Earth: How Hollywood, Big Labor, and Politicians Blacklisted a Movie in Cold War America*. Albuquerque: University of New Mexico Press.

MacEoin, Gary. 1985. *Sanctuary: A Resource Guide for Understanding and Participating in the Central American Refugees' Struggle*. San Francisco: Harper and Row.

Mahler, Kristin. 1995. *American Dreaming: Immigrant Life on the Margin*. Princeton, NJ: Princeton University Press.

Marshall, T.H. 1964 [1950]. *Citizenship and Social Class*. New York: Doubleday and Company.

Martínez, Martha A. 2009 "Promoting and Maintaining Home Ownership among Latino Immigrants." http://latinostudies.nd.edu/pubs/pubs/EsperanzaNo3_WEB.pdf. Accessed October 1, 2010.

Martínez-Saladaña, Jesús. 2004. "Building the Future: The FIOB and Civic Participation of Mexican Immigrants in Fresno, California." Pp. 125–43 in *Indigenous Mexican Migrants in the United States*, edited by Jonathan Fox and Gaspar Rivera-Salgado. La Jolla, CA: Center for US-Mexican Studies, UCSD and Center for Comparative Immigration Studies.

Massaldi, Julian. 2003. "Buenos Aires Consensus." Z Communications, November 20. http://www.zcommunications.org/buenos-aires-consensus-by-julian-massaldi. Accessed April 20, 2011.

Massey, Douglas (Ed.). 2008. *New Faces in New Places: The Changing Geography of American Immigration*. New York: Russell Sage Foundation.

Massey, Douglas, Rafael Alarcon, Jorge Durand and Humberto González. 1987.

References

Return to Aztlan: The Social Process of International Migration from Western Mexico. Berkeley: University of California Press.

McAdam, Douglas. 1990. *Freedom Summer.* New York: Oxford University Press.

McClure, Laura. 1995. "AFL-CIO: A New Era?" *Labor Notes* 201 (December): 10.

McDowell, Meghan G. and Nancy A. Wonders. 2009/10. "Keeping Migrants in their Place: Technologies of Control and Racialized Public Space in Arizona." *Social Justice* 36(2): 54–72.

McWilliams, Carey. 1990 [1948]. *The Spanish-Speaking People of the United States,* 2nd edition. New York: Praeger.

Menjívar, Cecilia. 1997. "Immigrant Kinship Networks and the Impact of the Receiving Context: Salvadorans in San Francisco in the Early 1990s." *Social Problems* 44(1): 104–23.

Meyerson, Harold. 2006. "The Power of the Numbers." *Washington Post,* A23.

Mignolo, Walter. 2005 *The Idea of Latin America.* New York: Blackwell.

Millard, Ann V. and Jorge Chapa. 2004. *Apple Pie and Enchiladas: Latino Newcomers in the Rural Midwest.* Austin: University of Texas Press.

Mines, Richard, Sandra Nichols and David Runsten. 2010. *California's Indigenous Farmworkers.* http://www.indigenousfarmworkers.org/IFS%20Full%20Report%20_Jan2010.pdf. Accessed April 20, 2011.

Mize, Ronald L. 1997. "The Life Story of Don Jorge de Colima." Fresno, California.

Mize, Ronald L., Aditi Mehta, Sarah Heath Olesiuk and Elias Saba. 2009. "Latino In-Migration among Counties in Decline: Evidence from 20 Upstate New York Counties." *CaRDI Rural New York Minute* 31 (July).

Mize, Ronald L. and Alicia C.S. Swords. 2010. *Consuming Mexican Labor: From the Bracero Program to NAFTA.* Toronto: University of Toronto Press.

Montejano, David. 1987. *Anglos and Mexicans in the Making of Texas.* Austin: University of Texas Press.

Morrow, Carol Ann. 2004. "The Coffee/Conscience Connection." *St. Anthony Messenger,* February 4. http://www.americancatholic.org/messenger/feb2004/feature1.asp. Accessed April 20, 2011.

Munley, James M. 2006. http://www.pamd.uscourts.gov/opinions/munley/06v1586-op.pdf. Accessed October 1, 2010.

Muñoz, Carlos Jr. 2003. *Youth, Identity, Power: The Chicano Movement.* New York: Verso.

Mydans, Seth. 1995. "A New Wave of Immigrants on the Lowest Rung in Farming." *The New York Times,* August 24. http://www.nytimes.com/1995/08/24/us/a-new-wave-of-immigrants-on-farming-s-lowest-rung.html. Accessed July 6, 2011.

Nevins, Joseph. 2002. *Dying to Live: A Story of U.S. Immigration in an Age of Global Apartheid?* San Francisco: Open Media/City Lights Books.

References

Ngai, Mae. 2004. *Impossible Subjects: Illegal Aliens and the Making of Modern America*. Princeton, NJ: Princeton University Press.

Omi, Michael and Howard Winant. 1994. *Racial Formation in the United States: From the 1960s to the 1990s*. New York: Routledge.

Oquendo, Angel R. 1998. "Re-imagining the Latino/a Race." Pp. 60–71 in *The Latino/a Condition: A Critical Reader*, edited by Richard Delgado and Jean Stefancic. New York: New York University Press.

Orozco, Cynthia E. 1995. "Beyond Machismo, la Familia, and Ladies Auxiliaries: A Historiography of Mexican-Origin Women's Participation in Voluntary Associations and Politics in the United States, 1870–1990." Pp. 1–34 in *Perspectives in Mexican American Studies*, edited by Juan García. Tucson: University of Arizona Press.

Orozco, Manuel. 2002. *Latino Hometown Associations as Agents of Development in Sending Money Home: Hispanic Remittances and Community Development*. New York: Rowman and Littlefield.

Ortman, Jennifer M. and Christine E. Guarnieri. 2009. *United States Population Predictions: 2000–2050*. Washington, DC: US Census Bureau. http://www.census.gov/population/www/projections/analytical-document09.pdf.

Padilla, Felix M. 1985. *Latino Ethnic Consciousness*. Notre Dame, IN: University of Notre Dame Press.

Park, Robert E. and Ernest Burgess. 1921. *Introduction to the Science of Society*. Chicago: University of Chicago Press.

Park, Robert E. and Herbert A. Miller. 1921. *Old World Traits Transplanted*. New York: Harper and Brothers Publishing.

Parra, Ricardo. 2004. "Latinos in the Midwest: Civil Rights and Community Action." In *Latinos in the Midwest: Civil Rights and Community Action*, edited by Gilberto Cárdenas. Houston: Arte Publico Press.

Passel, Jeffrey S. and D'Vera Cohn. 2008. *U.S. Population Predictions: 2005–2050*. Washington, DC: Pew Research Center. http://pewhispanic.org/files/reports/85.pdf.

Pawel, Miriam. 2009. *The Union of Their Dreams: Power, Hope, and Struggle in Cesar Chavez's Farm Worker Movement*. New York: Bloomsbury Press.

Pedraza, Silvia. 1981. "Cubans and Mexicans in the United States: The Functions of Political and Economic Migration." *Cuban Studies* 11/12: 79–97.

Pedraza, Silvia. 1985. *Political and Economic Migrants in America: Cubans and Mexicans*. Austin: University of Texas Press.

Peña, Devon. 1998. *Chicano Culture, Ecology, Politics: Subversive Kin*. Tucson: University of Arizona Press.

Peña, Devon. 2005. *Mexican Americans and the Environment: Tierra y Vida*. Tucson: University of Arizona Press.

Perea, Juan F. 1997. *Immigrants Out! The New Nativism and the Anti-Immigrant Impulse in the United States*. New York: New York University Press.

Pérez, Juan. 2004. *The Near Northwest Side Story: Migration, Displacement,*

References

and Puerto Rican Families. Berkeley, Los Angeles and London: University of California Press.

Police Department, County of Suffolk, New York. 2008a. "Written Statement of José Pacheco." http://www.longislandwins.com/downloads/20100409-Jose_Pachecos_Written_Statement.pdf. Accessed April 20, 2011.

Police Department, County of Suffolk, New York. 2008b. "Written Statement of Nicholas Hausch." http://www.longislandwins.com/downloads/20100323-hausch_state1.pdf. Accessed April 20, 2011.

Police Department, County of Suffolk, New York. 2008c. "Written Statement of Anthony Hartford." http://www.longislandwins.com/downloads/20100323-hartford_state1.pdf. Accessed April 20, 2011.

Portes, Alejandro and Robert Bach. 1985. *Latin Journey: Cuban and Mexican Immigrants in the United States*. Berkeley: University of California Press.

Portes, Alejandro, William Haller and Luis E. Guarnizo. 2002. "Transnational Entrepreneurs: An Alternative Form of Immigrant Economic Adaptation." *American Sociological Review* 67: 278–99.

Portes, Alejandro and Ruben Rumbaut. 2006. *Immigrant America: A Portrait*. Berkeley: University of California Press.

Portes, Alejandro and Alex Stepick. 1993. *City on the Edge: The Transformation of Miami*. Berkeley: University of California Press.

Portugues, Candida. 2009. "New Report about Deportations of Dominicans." *El Diario La Prensa*, translated by Emily Leavitt, May 1. http://www.indy-pressny.org/nycma/voices/371/news/news_2/. Accessed June 1, 2010.

Prewitt, Kenneth. 2005. "Racial Classification in America: Where Do We Go from Here?" *Daedalus* 134(1): 5–18.

Quijano, Anibal. 2000. "Coloniality of Power, Eurocentrism, and Latin America." *Nepantla* 1(3): 533–80.

Quinones, Sam. 2008. *Antonio's Gun and Delfino's Dream: Truer Tales of Mexican Migration*. Albuquerque: University of New Mexico Press.

Ramos Zayas, Ana. 2003. *National Performances: The Politics of Class, Race, and Space in Puerto Rican Chicago*. Chicago and London: University of Chicago Press.

Reimers, David M. 1992. *Still the Golden Door: The Third World Comes to America*. New York: Columbia University Press.

Renshon, Stanley. 2001. "Dual Citizenship and American National Identity." Center for Immigration Studies. http://www.cis.org/node/51. Accessed June 1, 2010.

Ricourt, Milagros and Ruby Danta. 2003. *Hispanas de Queens: Latino Panethnicity in a New York City Neighborhood*. Ithaca, NY: Cornell University Press.

Rodríguez, Ana P. 2005. "Departamento 15: Cultural Narratives of Salvadoran Transnational Migration." *Latino Studies* 3(1): 19–45.

References

Romero, Mary and Marwa Serag. 2005. "Violation of Latino Civil Rights Resulting from INS and Local Police's Use of Race, Culture and Class Profiling: The Case of the Chandler Roundup in Arizona." *Cleveland State Law Review* 52(1/2): 75–96.

Rosaldo, Renato. 1994. "Cultural Citizenship in San Jose, California." *PoLAR: Political and Legal Anthropology Review* 17(2): 57–64.

Rosaldo, Renato. 1997. "Cultural Citizenship, Inequality, and Multiculturalism." In *Latino Cultural Citizenship*, edited by William V. Flores and Rina Benmayor. Boston: Beacon Press.

Rouse, Roger. 1991. "Mexican Migration and the Social Space of Postmodernism." *Diaspora* 1: 8–23.

Rúa, Mérida M. 2006. "Latinidades." Pp. 505–7 in *Oxford Encyclopedia of Latinos and Latinas in the United States*, edited by Deena J. González and Suzanne Oboler. New York: Oxford University Press.

Ruiz, Vicki L. 1987. *Cannery Women, Cannery Lives: Mexican Women, Unionization, and the California Food Processing Industry, 1930–1950.* Albuquerque: University of New Mexico Press.

Rumbaut, Rubén. 1997. "Assimilation and its Discontents: Between Rhetoric and Reality." *International Migration Review* 31(4): 923–60.

Rumbaut, Rubén. 2009. "Pigments of our Imagination: On the Racialization and Racial Identities of Hispanics and Latinos." Pp. 15–36 in *How the United States Racializes Latinos: White Hegemony and its Consequences*, edited by José A. Cobas, Jorge Duany and Joe R. Feagin. Boulder, CO: Paradigm Publishers.

Sánchez, George. 1993. *Becoming Mexican American*. New York: Oxford University Press.

Sánchez-Korrol, Virginia. 1994. *From Colonia to Community: The History of Puerto Ricans in New York City*. Berkeley: University of California Press.

Sassen, Saskia. 1998. *Globalization and its Discontents: Essays on the New Mobility of People and Money*. New York: New Press.

Sassen, Saskia. 2001. *The Global City: New York, London, Tokyo*. Princeton, NJ: Princeton University Press.

Sassen, Saskia. 2005. "Global Cities and Processes." In *The Oxford Encyclopedia of Latinos and Latinas in the United States*, edited by Suzanne Oboler and Deena Gonzalez. New York: Oxford University Press.

Segura, Denise A. and Jennifer L. Pierce. 1993. "Chicana/o Family Structure and Gender Personality: Chodorow, Familism, and Psychoanalytic Sociology Revisited." *Signs: Journal of Women and Culture in Society* 19(1): 62–91.

Semple, Kirk. 2008. "A Killing in a Town Where Latinos Sense Hate." *The New York Times*, November 14.

Shafir, Gershon (Ed.). 1998. *The Citizenship Debates*. Minneapolis: University of Minnesota Press.

Shakira. 2010. "Arizona and Our Future," May 3. http://www.shakira.com.

References

Shaw, Randy. 2008. *Beyond the Fields: Cesar Chavez, the UFW, and the Struggle for Justice in the 21st Century.* Berkeley: University of California Press.

Singer, Audrey, Susan W. Hardwick and Caroline B. Brettell. 2008. *Twenty-First Century Gateways: Immigrant Incorporation in Suburban America.* Washington, DC: Brookings Institution Press.

Smith, Michael Peter and Matt Bakker. 2008. *Citizenship across Borders: The Political Transnationalism of El Migrante.* Ithaca, NY: Cornell University Press.

Smith, Robert C. 2006. *Mexican New York: Transnational Lives of New Immigrants.* Berkeley: University of California Press.

Sorrentino, Michael. 2010. "Sixth Teen Sentenced for Hate Crimes." *PatchoguePatch*, September 1. http://patchogue.patch.com/articles/sixth-teen-sentenced-for-hate-crimes. Accessed April 20, 2011.

Southern Poverty Law Center (SPLC). 2009. "Climate of Fear: Latino Immigrants in Suffolk County, N.Y.: A Special Report from the Southern Poverty Law Center, Montgomery, Alabama." http://www.splcenter.org/sites/default/files/downloads/publication/splc_suffolk_report.pdf. Accessed April 20, 2011.

Soysal, Yasemin Nuhoglu. 1994. *Limits of Citizenship: Migrants and Postnational Membership in Europe.* Chicago: University of Chicago Press.

Steinberg, Stephen. 1989. *The Ethnic Myth: Race, Ethnicity, and Class in America.* Boston: Beacon Press.

Stephen, Lynn. 2007. *Transborder Lives: Indigenous Oaxacans in Mexico, California, and Oregon.* Durham, NC: Duke University Press.

Stephen, Lynn, Patricia Zavella, Matthew C. Gutmann and Félix V. Matos-Rodríguez. 2003. "Introduction: Understanding the Américas: Insights from Latina/o and Latin American Studies." Pp. 1–32 in *Perspectives on Las Américas: A Reader in Culture, History and Representation*, edited by Matthew C. Gutmann, Félix V. Matos-Rodríguez, Lynn Stephen and Patricia Zavella. Malden, MA: Blackwell.

Storrs, K. Larry. 1987. "El Salvador Aid: Congressional Action, 1981–1986, on President Reagan's Requests for Economic and Military Assistance for El Salvador." Foreign Affairs and National Defense Division. Washington, DC: Congressional Research Service Publication 87-230.

Suro, Roberto and Audrey Singer. 2002. "Latino Growth in Metropolitan America: Changing Patterns, New Locations." The Brookings Institution Center on Urban and Metropolitan Policy and the Pew Hispanic Center. http://www.brook.edu/es/urban/publications/surosinger.pdf. Accessed October 15, 2010.

Swords, Alicia C. and Ronald L. Mize. 2008. "Beyond Tourist Gazes and Performances: U.S. Consumption of Land and Labor in Puerto Rican and Mexican Destinations." *Latin American Perspectives* 35(3): 53–69.

Takaki, Ronald. 1993. *A Different Mirror: A History of Multicultural America.* New York: Little, Brown and Company.

References

Taylor, Charles. 1994. *Multiculturalism: Examining the Politics of Recognition.* Princeton, NJ: Princeton University Press.

Telles, Edward E. and Vilma Ortiz. 2008. *Generations of Exclusion: Mexican Americans, Assimilation, and Race.* New York: Russell Sage Foundation.

The New York Times. 2008. "A Death in Patchogue." November 11.

Thomas, W.I. and Florian Znaniecki. 1984 [1918–20]. *The Polish Peasant in Europe and America: Monograph of an Immigrant Group.* Boston: The Gorham Press.

Torras, Mariano and Curtis Skinner. 2010. "The Economic Impact of the Hispanic Population on Long Island, New York: A Research Report Prepared for the Horace Hagedorn Foundation." http://www.hagedornfoundation.org/downloads/Adelphi%20Report.pdf. Accessed April 20, 2011.

Trotsky, Leon. 1980 [1932]. *The History of the Russian Revolution.* New York: Pathfinder.

US Census Bureau. 2000a. *1990 and 2000 Summary Tape File 1*

US Census Bureau. 2000b. *Census of Population and Housing.*

US Census Bureau. 2009. *American Community Survey, 2006–2008 Three-Year Estimates.*

US Department of Homeland Security (DHS). 2010. "Temporary Protected Status." http://www.uscis.gov/portal/site/uscis/menuitem.eb1d4c2a3e5b9ac89243c6a7543f6d1a/?vgnextoid=848f7f2ef0745210VgnVCM100000082ca60aRCRD&vgnextchannel=848f7f2ef0745210VgnVCM100000082ca60aRCRD. Accessed July 6, 2011.

US Department of Labor (DOL). 2009. "The Foreign Labor Certification Report: 2009 Data, Trends and Highlights Across Programs and States." http://www.foreignlaborcert.doleta.gov/pdf/2009_Annual_Report.pdf. Accessed December 1, 2010.

Vargas, Zaragosa. 1997. "*Tejana* Radical: Emma Tenayuca and the San Antonio Labor Movement during the Great Depression." *Pacific Historical Review* 66(4): 553–80.

Waldinger, Roger. 1996. "From Ellis Island to LAX: Immigrant Prospects in the American City." *International Migration Review* 30: 1078–86.

Whalen, Carmen T. 2001. *From Puerto Rico to Philadelphia: Puerto Rican Workers and Postwar Economies.* Philadelphia: Temple University Press.

Zúñiga, Víctor and Rubén Hernández-León (Eds). 2006. *New Destinations: Mexican Immigration in the United States.* New York: Russell Sage Foundation.

Index

Index

Index

Index